W9-CUH-816

"In this book, Jerry Bridges does what he does best: teaches us how to think rightly about holiness and spiritual formation. He starts and ends with the gospel so that through it we learn of both our need for holiness and the way by which we are conformed to the image of Christ. As always, Jerry takes this foundation of right thinking to application, clearly laying out how we are to go about living holy lives. Because of his sincere devotion to the study of Scripture and holy living, there is no one today more trustworthy to read on this subject than Jerry."

— REVEREND WILLIAM VOGLER, pastor,
Grace Evangelical Presbyterian Church, Lawrence, Kansas;
moderator of the 27th General Assembly of the
Evangelical Presbyterian Church

"Jerry Bridges has marvelously, attractively, and clearly communicated in this informative and inspirational treatise that God's saving grace in Christ invites us to come just as we are. This book should be not only read and absorbed personally but also used to share with others as an excellent instrument of life-changing disciple-making."

— HARRY L. REEDER, III, pastor and teacher,
Briarwood Presbyterian Church, Birmingham, Alabama

"Jerry Bridges tells us what we must never forget: God's ultimate purpose for His people is to conform them to the image of His Son. Combining his characteristic brevity and lucidity, Bridges reminds us why it matters and how it is accomplished."

— ALISTAIR BEGG, pastor, Parkside Church, Chagrin Falls, Ohio

"If you cut Jerry Bridges, he bleeds Bible. In a day when there is so much confusion about grace, Jerry shows how a true understanding of grace is the only sure foundation for spiritual transformation. This book is essential reading for those who want to know how to pursue holiness and live by grace without resorting to legalistic self-effort. As a pastor, this is the book I want my people to read in order to get a biblical view of how to grow in holiness and joy."

— REVEREND MARK BATES, senior pastor,
Village Seven Presbyterian Church, Colorado Springs, Colorado

"Jerry Bridges gets the gospel. He knows how it transforms unbeliever and believer alike, and his life mission is to ensure that we know it as well. This book is Bridges' latest installment exalting in a gospel that is both glorious and profoundly functional for everyday life. I'm grateful he's given us this gift, and I'm eager to pass it on to friends and family to encourage them."

— DAVE HARVEY, author of *Rescuing Ambition*;
church planter, Sovereign Grace Ministries

The
TRANSFORMING
POWER
of the
GOSPEL

For our sake he made him to be sin who knew no sin,
so that in him we might
become the righteousness of God.

2 CORINTHIANS 5:21

JERRY BRIDGES

NAVPRESS

Discipleship Inside Out™

Discipleship Inside Out™

NavPress is the publishing ministry of The Navigators, an international Christian organization and leader in personal spiritual development. NavPress is committed to helping people grow spiritually and enjoy lives of meaning and hope through personal and group resources that are biblically rooted, culturally relevant, and highly practical.

**For a free catalog go to www.NavPress.com
or call 1.800.366.7788 in the United States or 1.800.839.4769 in Canada.**

© 2012 by Jerry Bridges

ISBN-13: 978-1-61747-922-9 (hardback); 978-1-61291-164-9 (paperback)

Cover design by studiogearbox
Cover images by Nat Photos/Getty

Some of the anecdotal illustrations in this book are true to life and are included with the permission of the persons involved. All other illustrations are composites of real situations, and any resemblance to people living or dead is coincidental.

Unless otherwise identified, all Scripture quotations in this publication are taken from The Holy Bible, English Standard Version (ESV), copyright © 2001 by Crossway Bibles, a division of Good News Publishers. Used by permission. All rights reserved. Other versions used include: the Holy Bible, New International Version® (NIV®). Copyright © 1973, 1978, 1984 by Biblica, used by permission of Zondervan; the New American Standard Bible® (NASB), Copyright © 1960, 1962, 1963, 1968, 1971, 1972, 1973, 1975, 1977, 1995 by The Lockman Foundation. Used by permission; and the King James Version (KJV).

Bridges, Jerry.
  The transforming power of the Gospel / Jerry Bridges.
    p. cm.
  Includes bibliographical references (p.   ).
  ISBN 978-1-61747-922-9
  1. Sanctification—Christianity. 2. Christian life. I. Title.
  BT765.B8 2012
  234'.8—dc23
                              2011034259

Printed in the United States of America

1 2 3 4 5 6 7 8 / 17 16 15 14 13 12

Dedicated to the memory of

William Jackson Bridges
1926–2005

Faithful Servant of Jesus Christ

and a

True Older Brother

"He . . . served his own generation by the will of God."
ACTS 13:36 (KJV)

Contents

Preface

Spiritual transformation is the process through which we grow more and more into the likeness of Christ. Since 1951, when I first came in contact with The Navigators ministry, I have sought to understand and live out the principles of that process. I have by no means "arrived," either in understanding or application, but I have learned a lot and hopefully have grown some over these sixty years.

Early in the 1970s, God opened opportunities to teach informally what I was learning, first with The Navigators and later to a wider audience in the United States. Then I was invited to teach at several seminaries and Christian colleges. These opportunities required a more disciplined approach to what I was teaching, and I eventually developed a curriculum of twenty to twenty-five lectures, depending on the requirements of the school. In order to reach a wider audience, I condensed that material into ten lectures to be given during a two-day seminar. This book is essentially that seminar in written form.

I do not submit this book as a comprehensive work on spiritual transformation. For one thing, it does not include all that I have written in other books such as *The Pursuit of Holiness* or *Transforming Grace*. And there are other contemporary writers who have approached this subject from different angles and have much to say to us.

Why then this book? The answer is to teach what I have learned more deeply in the last twenty-five years about the importance of the gospel in our transformation and the vital necessity of the work of the Holy Spirit in the process.

I gladly acknowledge that I stand on the shoulders (though somewhat precariously) of some of the great giants of the faith of previous centuries. That is why you will find numerous quotations from them. I hope their words, in addition to the many Scriptures cited, will give you confidence that what I have written is not new and novel but is essentially the teaching of Scripture and is consistent with the teachings of these respected men of the last four centuries.

I want to acknowledge with gratitude the help of several people. First is my wife, Jane, who patiently endured many occasions of frustration as I struggled to put into concise words the thoughts in my head. Then Don Simpson, a personal friend and senior editor at NavPress, who has worked with me chapter by chapter as the book was being written with both helpful suggestions and the encouragement I so often needed.

Connie Trautman, my part-time administrative assistant, typed and retyped my handwritten copy into digital format on the computer. Bob Bevington, Chris Thifault, and the Reverend Bill Vogler read the initial draft of the manuscript and offered helpful suggestions. Bob also wrote the discussion questions at the end of each chapter. Finally, but by no means least in importance, a number of friends prayed for me during the months of the writing process.

Most of all, I thank God the Father who, by His grace and through the Lord Jesus Christ and with the help of the Holy Spirit, gave me the privilege of writing this book. To the triune God be all the glory for any usefulness this book may have among God's people.

CHAPTER ONE

Too Soon Old, Too Late Smart

Not that I have already obtained this or am already perfect, but I press on to make it my own, because Christ Jesus has made me his own. Brothers, I do not consider that I have made it my own. But one thing I do: forgetting what lies behind and straining forward to what lies ahead, I press on toward the goal for the prize of the upward call of God in Christ Jesus.

PHILIPPIANS 3:12-14

God has predestined all believers to be conformed to the image of His Son (see Romans 8:29). The process toward that goal is called by various names such as sanctification, growth in grace, or transformation (see 1 Thessalonians 5:23-24; 2 Peter 3:18; 2 Corinthians 3:18). This process of transformation into the image of Christ begins at our new birth (see John 3:3-5) and continues until we die and enter into the presence of the Lord. At that time, according to Hebrews 12:23, our spirits will be made perfect. The transformation process will be completed.

Not only has God predestined us to be transformed into the image of His Son, He has commanded us to be transformed. Through the apostle Paul, God said, "Do not be conformed to this world, but be transformed by the renewal of your mind"

(Romans 12:2). In a similar way, the apostle Peter wrote, "As obedient children, do not be conformed to the passions of your former ignorance, but as he who called you is holy, you also be holy in all your conduct, since it is written, 'You shall be holy, for I am holy'" (1 Peter 1:14-16).

To be transformed into the image of God's Son and to be holy as God is holy are essentially synonymous expressions. But what I want us to see through these similar expressions is that what God has predestined for us, He commands us to pursue. There is no conflict between God's sovereign will, which He will certainly accomplish, and His moral will for us, which we are to pursue.

This transformation into the image of Jesus is much more than a change of outward conduct; rather, it is a deep penetrating work of the Holy Spirit in the very core of our being, what the Bible calls the heart — the center of our intellect, affections, and will. It is what is sometimes called "a change from the inside out."

But though the transformation process is primarily the work of the Holy Spirit, it very much involves our earnest, active pursuit of that holiness without which no one will see the Lord (see Hebrews 12:14). So what is it that will engage our affections or desires to earnestly pursue transformation into the likeness of Jesus? What is it that will inspire us to *want* to do what we *ought* to do? This is a major question that we'll seek to answer in chapter 6. Its answer is one of the key lessons I have learned in my own journey toward spiritual transformation.

MY JOURNEY

My journey began at age eighteen when I asked Jesus to be my Savior. Having grown up in church, and even considering myself to be a Christian, I was essentially a good kid and never strayed beyond the moral boundaries of my church. I had no major sins that I needed to put away, so the transformation process in my life was at first slow and almost imperceptible. In fact, looking back after sixty years, I now realize I did not know I needed to be transformed. After all, I was living a decent moral life and was not committing the more obvious sins of many of my fellow students at college.

An event one night in January 1952 changed that dramatically. That night, due to a statement I heard at Bible study, I realized that the Bible was meant to be applied in a practical way to my daily life. As a result, on the way back to my ship (I was a young officer in the U.S. Navy at the time), I prayed a simple prayer: "God, starting tonight, would You use the Bible to guide my conduct?" That was the day my own spiritual transformation really got under way.

There is an old proverb that says, "Too soon old, too late smart." That proverb describes my transformation journey. I think I've made most of the theological mistakes in the realm of spiritual transformation, due to my own ignorance and the lack of solid Bible teaching in those early days. (I was at sea most of the time and, to my knowledge, the only Christian aboard my ship.)

The first mistake I made was assuming I could live the Christian life by my own moral willpower. "Just read what the Bible says and do it." I was used to obeying orders from my superior officers, and I approached the moral commands of the Bible the same way. I knew nothing of the internal fighting between the flesh and the Spirit. I did not realize the necessity of relying on the Holy Spirit to enable me to apply the Scriptures to my life. After several years of this self-effort approach, I grew discouraged over the prospects of seeing significant change in my life. While still not involved in any of the so-called "major" sins, I was seeing the subtle, often hidden sins of the heart. I seemed to be getting worse, not better. This set me up for the next mistake, the embracing of a passive approach to spiritual transformation.

Known by various descriptive phrases such as "higher life" and "deeper life" and by slogans such as "Let go and let God" and "Just trust Jesus to live His life through you," this totally passive approach taught that just as you can do nothing for your salvation but trust in Jesus, so you can do nothing for your transformation but trust in Jesus. Obviously after the discouragement of the "Do it yourself" approach, this seemed to be good news, almost a second chapter to the gospel of salvation. Instead it turned out to be even more discouraging because over time it was quite obvious to me that Jesus was not living His life through me. Instead I found myself battling the same old sins of the heart that I had struggled with before.

God in His mercy rescued me from this passive approach and enabled me to see what I now believe to be the biblical approach, and of course that is what this book is all about. But in the course of those years of struggle, I learned three valuable lessons:

1. The internal warfare between the flesh and the Spirit that Paul described in Galatians 5:17 is the normal Christian life. Regardless of how much we grow spiritually, we will all our lives experience the conflict between the desires of the flesh and the desires of the Spirit.

2. The more we grow in Christlikeness, the more sin we will see in our lives. It isn't that we are sinning more; rather we are growing more aware of and more sensitive to sin that has been there all along. The Holy Spirit does not reveal all our sins of the heart to us at once. Instead He brings us along gradually as He works to transform us into the image of Christ.

3. Spiritual transformation requires of us what I call dependent responsibility. All the moral commands and exhortations of Scripture assume our responsibility. We cannot "just let Jesus live His life through me." No, we

are responsible. At the same time, we are dependent on the Holy Spirit to both do His own work and enable us through His power to do the work we must do.

In 1978, my first book, *The Pursuit of Holiness*, was published. The three valuable lessons I just described were incorporated into that book, and God has graciously blessed its ministry far beyond anything I could have imagined. But I still had more to learn.

If it is true that the more we grow, the more sin we see in our lives, what will keep us from becoming discouraged? The answer is the realization that both our eternal salvation and our day-to-day standing with God are based not on our own performance but upon the sinless life and sin-bearing death of Jesus. (This will be developed more fully in chapter 5 of this book.)

As I began to pursue this truth, I saw to a greater extent how the gospel (that is, the message of what Christ has done for us and continues to do) provides both the foundation and motivation for our role in spiritual transformation, what I call our "pursuit of holiness." As I studied the Scriptures regarding the role of the gospel in our transformation, God also graciously brought to my attention, through various means, the writings of some of the great teachers of earlier centuries, dating back to the days of the Reformation. I saw how consistently these men taught that the gospel is the foundation for our transformation. This, then, has become a major theme in my ministry.

Before I understood the gospel's important role in our transformation, I thought it was only for unbelievers. Once we became believers, we didn't need it anymore except to share with those who still were unbelievers. I thought all we needed as Christians were the challenges and "how to" of discipleship. After all, Jesus said to go and make disciples of all nations (see Matthew 28:19).

We do need challenge and instruction in discipleship, but we also need the gospel every day in our lives because we still sin every day of our lives. And, as I have already said, the more we grow, the more we see our sin. But because we are performance oriented by nature and our culture enforces that orientation, we want to somehow relate to God every day on the basis of our perceived performance. If we've been good, as we would define goodness, we feel reasonably secure in our relationship with God. If, on the other hand, we've had a "bad day" spiritually, we tend to feel insecure. In fact, that insecurity may cause us to live in denial of how bad our bad days really are.

But we cannot grow spiritually if we do not see our need to grow. And if our insecurity about our day-to-day relationship with God causes us to live in denial about our sin, we will not grow. This is one reason we still need the gospel every day. It helps us move from a performance relationship with God to one based on the sinless life and sin-bearing death of Jesus Christ. It daily reminds us that from God's point of view, our relationship with Him is not based on how good or bad we've been but upon the perfect goodness and death of our Lord Jesus Christ. Thus, the gospel frees us up to honestly face our sin, knowing that because of Christ's death, God no longer counts that sin against us (see Romans 4:7-8).

The aim of this book is to serve God's goal that we become more conformed to the image of His Son. The structure of the book basically is two parts. In the second part, we will look at the work of the Holy Spirit in our transformation and how we are to relate to Him in our "dependent responsibility." In the first part, we will look more closely at the role of the gospel. However, because the gospel is only for sinners, yes even for us who are still practicing sinners, we will consider the seriousness of even our more subtle or "refined" sins. But the seriousness of our sin can be seen only in the light of the infinite holiness of God. So we will begin our studies in spiritual transformation with a look at God's holiness and the implications of that holiness for us.

FOR GROUP DISCUSSION

1. Spiritual transformation requires dependent responsibility. How does this differ from living by the concept of "Let go and let God"?
2. If we live in denial about our sin, we will not grow. How does the gospel free us up to honestly face our sin?
3. Why do believers in Christ still need the gospel every day?

The Holiness of God

*In the year that King Uzziah died I saw the Lord sitting upon
a throne, high and lifted up; and the train of his robe filled the
temple. Above him stood the seraphim. Each had six wings: with
two he covered his face, and with two he covered his feet, and with
two he flew. And one called to another and said: "Holy, holy, holy
is the* LORD *of hosts; the whole earth is full of his glory!"*

ISAIAH 6:1-3

The Hebrew language uses repetition to indicate emphasis as
we do by italics or boldface type. Jesus used this device when
He would preface a statement with "Truly, truly I say to you" (for
example, see John 3:3; 5:24). The Bible, however, uses a threefold
repetition, "Holy, holy, holy," with reference to God and His
holiness. Such a threefold repetition in Hebrew indicates the
highest possible degree or, as we could say, the infiniteness of
God's holiness.

What is infinite? The distance to the known edge of the universe is said to be about thirteen billion light-years away. Stated in
miles, that would be about 78,000,000,000,000,000,000,000.
To save you counting, that is twenty-one zeros! Seventy-eight
billion, trillion miles. That is an exceedingly vast distance, but it
is not an infinite distance. Infinite means without limits and
immeasurable. Only God is infinite, and He is infinite in all His

glorious attributes. But it is only His holiness that is given the threefold ascription "holy, holy, holy." We never read of God's being "wise, wise, wise" or "powerful, powerful, powerful," though He is infinite in all His attributes. It appears that God purposed to magnify His holiness in a unique way. In fact, God's name is qualified by the adjective *holy* in the Old Testament more often than all other qualities put together.[1]

Because we cannot fully grasp the concept of infinity, God condescends to use relative terms of vastness or exceedingly great to speak to us of His infiniteness. For example, He says of Himself in Isaiah 40:15,17,

> Behold, the nations are like a drop from a bucket,
>   and are accounted as the dust on the scales....
> All the nations are as nothing before him,
>   they are accounted by him as less than nothing
>   and emptiness.

God is saying to us that because He is infinitely great, all the combined power and might of all the great nations and empires throughout history are to Him as less than nothing and emptiness. But we could multiply that combined power and might a thousand times and it would still be to God no more than a drop from a bucket. That is because He is infinite in an absolute sense, without limits or immeasurable. And this is the way we should understand the infinite holiness of God.

This emphasis on the infiniteness of God's holiness begs the question "What does the Bible mean when it speaks of the holiness of God?" The Hebrew word translated as holy is *qadosh*, which basically means "separate." Old Testament scholar E. J. Young says that *qadosh* signifies the entirety of the divine perfection that separates God from His creation, including His complete separation from all that is sinful.[2]

Holiness, when used of God, is a comprehensive term to denote all that God is in His transcendent majesty and infinite moral purity. Isaiah's vision of God, as recorded in Isaiah 6:1-8, is the classic passage of Scripture on the holiness of God, and it will help us gain insight into the holiness of God and the implication of that holiness for us today.

TRANSCENDENT MAJESTY

In his vision of God, Isaiah gave us three descriptive phrases about Him:

- He is sitting upon a throne.
- He is high and lifted up.
- The train of His robe fills the temple.

God's throne is symbolic of His reign or His sovereign rulership. God absolutely rules over all His creation in both the heavenly and physical realms. A sparrow cannot fall to the ground apart from His will (see Matthew 10:29). We cannot carry out the plans we make apart from His will (see James 4:13-15). By contrast, He does according to His will among the host of heaven and among the inhabitants of the earth (see Daniel 4:35). And in His sovereign authority as Creator, God has the absolute right to set the rules of conduct for His moral creatures, enforce those rules, and act as the supreme judge of all moral beings, rewarding good and punishing evil.

The expression "high and lifted up" speaks of His supreme exaltation — the glorious display of His royalty, splendor, and glory. The train of His robe filling the temple accentuates His royalty and splendor. With present-day bridal gowns, the train is the apex of the dress, indicating to some degree the beauty and expensiveness of the gown. Even more telling is the fact that the coronation robe of a king or queen always includes a train, the length of it intended to display the royalty and splendor of the person being crowned. When Queen Elizabeth II of Great Britain was crowned in 1953, her train was thirty-six feet long. It was made of velvet and trimmed in expensive ermine and was so heavy it had to be carried by six maids of honor, walking behind her.

By contrast, the train of God's robe was so long it filled the temple, an expression intended to convey to us the infinite royalty, splendor, dignity, and majesty of God. The royalty and splendor of the wealthiest and most powerful monarch who has ever lived is no more than a trifle compared to the royalty and splendor of God.

What we see then in Isaiah 6:1 is a picture of the transcendent majesty of God. The word *transcendent* means all-surpassing, above and beyond anything else. The word *majesty* includes all of God's sovereign power and authority, royalty, dignity, and splendor. So transcendent majesty speaks of the infinite power, authority, royalty, dignity, and splendor that is God's.

One of the earliest recorded references to the holiness of God occurs in the song of Moses after the Israelites had crossed the Red Sea and had seen God drown the Egyptian army in the sea. They sang, "Who is like you, O LORD, among the gods? Who is like you, majestic in holiness, awesome in glorious deeds, doing wonders?" (Exodus 15:11).

Note the phrase "majestic in holiness." In the context of the Red Sea episode, this is a reference to God's sovereign power and authority, specifically the power to deliver the Israelite people from the pursuit of the mighty Egyptian army. Consider what a stupendous act it was that God did in parting the Red Sea so that the Israelites could pass through. He caused the waters to part and stand up like concrete walls and made the sea bottom as dry land for the Israelites to walk on (see Exodus 14:21-29). And then through His same sovereign power, God released the parted waters to resume their normal course so the entire Egyptian army was drowned in the midst of the sea. No wonder the Israelites sang, "Who is like you, O LORD, among the gods?" (15:11).

Transcendent majesty is the first meaning of God's holiness. Isaiah, writing his book under the direct guidance of the Holy Spirit, used the phrase "Holy One of Israel" thirty times. In each instance, it is the infinite, transcendent majesty, power, and authority of God that is mostly in view. If we fail to grasp this idea and its implications to us, we will not grasp the weightiness of the second meaning of God's holiness, that of His infinite moral purity.

INFINITE MORAL PURITY

Isaiah not only *saw* God in His transcendent majesty, he also *heard* the seraphim calling out, "Holy, holy, holy is the LORD of hosts; the whole earth is full of his glory!" (Isaiah 6:3).[3] Isaiah would have known that *qadosh* means "separate," and he would have rightly understood that God is separate from us in His transcendent majesty. But he would also have remembered that when God was forming the people of Israel into a nation, He said to them, "You shall therefore be holy, for I am holy" (Leviticus 11:45).

Obviously when God says, "Be holy, for I am holy," He is not speaking of His transcendent majesty, which is reserved exclusively for Himself. Rather, He is referring to His infinite moral purity. It is only this aspect of His holiness that we can seek to emulate, even to only a small degree.

Recall again that the threefold repetition, "Holy, holy, holy," indicates the highest possible degree, or the infiniteness of God's holiness. So God is infinite not only in His majesty but also in His moral purity. This twofold aspect of God's holiness has profound implications for us, as we will see in the next chapter. But for now we can see that God's transcendent majesty adds weight to His moral purity, and His moral purity adds beauty to His majesty. We have a saying that "power corrupts, and absolute power corrupts absolutely." This may be true in a general sense of human rulers or politicians, but it is certainly not true of God. Rather, He is absolute in His power and infinite in His moral purity.

It is difficult for us to conceive of God's perfect moral purity because we always measure moral purity by a standard outside ourselves. But God is the standard, and when measured against the standard of God's infinite holiness, our own holiness on our very best day is no more than a drop in a bucket compared to His. In fact, Isaiah, toward the end of his book, went further and described all our righteous deeds as "like a polluted garment" (64:6).

Yet God has called us to be holy as He is holy. He has in effect called us to an impossible task. That is why Martin Luther, in the days before his understanding of the gospel, was so angry with God. In fact, once when asked if he loved God, he is said to have replied, "Love God? I hate God!" He realized that God was calling him to an impossible standard and then would damn him eternally for his failure to achieve it.

Impossible though it is for us to fulfill this standard, God has nevertheless called us to be holy as He is holy, and in order that we might understand what it means to be holy as He is holy, He has given to us His law (and here I am using *law* as a shorthand expression for all the moral will of God found throughout Scripture). God's law is both an expression of His moral will for us and also a reflection of His character. Remember, though, who it is that has said, "Be holy for I am holy." It is the infinite sovereign ruler of all creation, who has both the power to rule and the sovereign authority to require obedience to His law. We should always keep in mind this twofold aspect of God's holiness: His transcendent majesty and His infinite moral purity.

HATRED OF SIN

The combination of God's sovereign authority and His infinite moral purity leads to a third truth about God's holiness: His infinite hatred of all sin — that is, everything in His creation that is contradictory to His own holiness.

Habakkuk, in 1:13, said of God, "You who are of purer eyes than to see evil and cannot look at wrong." That is, God cannot look at evil with complacency or indifference. Rather, as Proverbs 6:16 says, "There are six things the LORD hates, seven that are an abomination to him." Note the words *hate* and *abomination*. Those are strong words, indicating God's infinite detestation of all sin, whether a major sin, such as adultery, or a more "acceptable sin," such as unkind words about someone else. Obviously there are degrees of sin, but our sins of pride, selfishness, jealousy, gossip, and the like are still sin. They are an abomination to Him.

The apostle Paul wrote in Romans 1:18, "The wrath of God is revealed from heaven against all ungodliness and unrighteousness." This is just one of several places in the New Testament that speaks of the wrath of God (see also John 3:36; Romans 2:5; Ephesians 2:3; Revelation 6:15-17). Of course, God's wrath is not a display of sinful emotions such as we usually associate with human wrath; rather it reflects His holy hatred of all sin and His determination to punish it. We might say that God's wrath is His infinite justice in action — a justice that cannot allow any sin, be it ever so small in our eyes, to go unpunished.

Our next chapter is on the subject of our sin, and we can see sin rightly only when we see it as against an infinitely holy God. Nineteenth-century writer William Plumer said, "All sin is against God in this sense; that it is His law that is broken, His authority that is despised, His government that is set at naught."[4] We may harm someone physically or damage his reputation through gossip, but what matters most of all is that it is God's law that we have violated.

Another nineteenth-century theologian wrote,

> The guilt of the offense is proportional to the greatness, the moral excellence, and the glory of Him against whom the offense is committed, and who made us for loyal obedience to Himself. Nothing else, therefore, comes into consideration in estimating the enormity of sin but the infinite majesty, glory and claims of Him against whom we sin.[5]

Suppose you want a new rug to cover the wooden floor in your living room. Being of modest means, you go the local discount store and pay three hundred dollars for a rug. I come into your house with a bottle of black indelible ink and spill that ink on your rug. I have just ruined your three-hundred-dollar rug. But suppose you are a wealthy person and you pay thirty thousand dollars for an expensive Persian rug. If I spill ink on that rug, it is an entirely different matter. Why is that true? It is the same act on my part. In both instances, I have spilled black indelible ink on a rug. The difference, of course, lies in the value of the rug.[6]

This is the way we should view the enormity of our sin. God's holiness cannot be compared to even the thirty-thousand-dollar rug. It is infinite. It is immeasurable. Furthermore, we do not accidently "spill" our sin on God's holiness. For the most part, we rather *pour* out our sin; that is, we choose to act out our pride and selfishness, our judgmental attitudes, and our unkind words about others. And when we do that, we deliberately pour out our sin on the holiness of God. That is why our sin, be it ever so small in our eyes, is always an abomination to God.

We need to be clear in our minds that the pursuit of holiness — that is, seeking to be holy as God is holy — is no light, incidental matter. It is central to the Christian life. The psalmist wrote, "You have commanded your precepts to be kept diligently" (Psalm 119:4). Diligently! That is the way we are to respond to God's command "Be holy, for I am holy" (1 Peter 1:16).

Yet in spite of God's holiness — that is, His sovereign authority and moral purity — few Christians give serious attention to the pursuit of holiness. In fact, most of us seem to be quite satisfied with our character and conduct if we live generally decent lives and avoid the scandalous sins of society around us. For this reason, we need to closely examine the seriousness of our sin or, as one of the Puritan writers so quaintly put it, the "sinfulness of our sin." And this we will do in the next chapter.

FOR GROUP DISCUSSION

1. When thinking about the holiness of God, why is it necessary to grasp the meaning of His transcendent majesty before we can understand His moral purity?
2. Do you think Christians tend to believe Isaiah's declaration that "all our righteous deeds are like a polluted garment"? Why or why not?
3. In view of God's transcendent majesty and infinite moral purity, why is His wrath necessary?

CHAPTER THREE

The Sinfulness
of Our Sin

I said: "Woe is me! For I am lost; for I am a man of unclean lips,
and I dwell in the midst of a people of unclean lips;
for my eyes have seen the King, the LORD of hosts!"

ISAIAH 6:5

We use the words *macro* and *micro* rather commonly to speak of the very great and very small. Then with computers, we have microprocessors and processing speeds in terms of microseconds, which is one-millionth of a second. Then I began to hear of speeds in terms of nanoseconds, which is one-billionth of a second. I say all this to say that in 1960, I had a nano (meaning one-billionth in intensity) experience of the holiness of God when compared to Isaiah's experience. It was through reading some of the Puritan Stephen Charnock's book *The Existence and Attributes of God.*

Having received Charnock's book as a gift, and because I knew that God had said, "You shall be holy because I am holy," I turned immediately to Charnock's chapter on the holiness of God. I began reading, and after only a few pages, I suddenly found myself on my knees before God because I was so overwhelmed by a sense of my own sinfulness before this holy God I was reading about. I got up and began reading again and soon found myself again on my knees before God.

I think of that experience some fifty years ago every time I read Isaiah 6:1-8. If just reading about God's holiness in a book written by a mere man had such an impact on me, I cannot imagine the overwhelming impact an actual God-given vision to Isaiah of God's holiness must have had on him. That's why I say that my own experience surely was no more than a nano experience of what Isaiah experienced.

ISAIAH'S RESPONSE

Isaiah was a member of the upper class, probably even elite class, of the people of Israel. We know he had access to the kings. He was undoubtedly a righteous man, in the same sense that Zechariah and Elizabeth, the parents of John the Baptist, were "righteous before God, walking blamelessly in all the commandments and statutes of the Lord" (Luke 1:6).

Yet here he cried out in desperation, "Woe is me, for I am lost, for I am a man of unclean lips" (Isaiah 6:5). Isaiah is the prophet of woe. In chapter 5, he pronounced woe six times. Now he pronounced it on himself. The word *unclean* he used is the same word lepers were required to use as they would cry out "unclean, unclean" (Leviticus 13:45).

Isaiah's vision occurred in the year that King Uzziah died. Uzziah had started his reign as a good king (see 2 Chronicles 26:4-5). But when he grew strong, he sinned against God by burning incense on the altar of incense in the temple, a function reserved for only the priests who were consecrated to burn incense. As a result, God struck him with leprosy and he was a leper to the day of his death, living isolated in a separate house and excluded from the temple.

Isaiah then, seeing this vision of God in the year of Uzziah's death, would have been keenly aware of the religious significance of leprosy for the people of Israel. So in crying out, "I am a man of unclean lips," he was essentially calling himself a moral leper. How could this be? How could a man who was presumably righteous before God call himself a moral leper? Because he had seen a vision of the infinite holiness of God and, by comparison, saw himself as a man of unclean lips. It would be this same comparison that would cause him to later write those memorable words "We have all become like one who is *unclean* [the same word as in Isaiah 6:5], and all our righteous deeds are like a polluted garment" (Isaiah 64:6).

For us today, this is where spiritual transformation really begins — when we begin to see that even our best deeds on our best days are like a polluted garment before an infinitely holy God.

Why "unclean lips"? Why not an unclean heart? Some say it was because he could not join the seraphim in their song of praise to God because they are sinless and he is sinful. That may be true, but I think there is still another reason. Most commentators on Isaiah consider Isaiah 6 God's initial call to Isaiah to the prophetic office. In this reasoning, Isaiah, in chapters 1–5, gave us a picture of the sinful environment into which he was called to be a prophet before he described his call. Note that in Isaiah 1:4 and again in 5:24, the people are described as those who have despised the Holy One of Israel or despised the Word of the Holy One of Israel.

So Isaiah's vision of God and the subsequent call (see 6:8-13) is actually his call to the office of prophet. And what is the primary instrument of a prophet? It is his lips, and Isaiah needs to be made painfully aware that he is not fit to be a prophet. He could be likened to a surgeon preparing to do a delicate surgery only to discover that his instruments are not just unclean but filthy. Isaiah has been made acutely and painfully aware of his sinfulness centering on his unclean lips, not because he is a wicked person but because he has seen his sin in the light of the holiness of God.

WHAT IS SIN?

What is sin? In our culture today, people no longer sin; they make mistakes. A prominent athlete had used performance-enhancing supplements. When confronted, she at first denied it until she could no longer do so. Later in a TV interview, the interviewer said to her, "You lied, didn't you?" to which the athlete said, "I made a *mistake*."

A prominent politician committed adultery with one of his staff members. When confronted, he said, "I made a serious error of judgment. I recognized my *mistake*." Another prominent person, a father who describes himself as "pro-choice" on the subject of abortion, said, "If one of my daughters made a *mistake*, I wouldn't want her to be saddled with a baby."

So in our broader culture, people no longer sin; they make mistakes. What about our Christian environment? In our case, sin is not denied. Instead it is often redefined to refer to the more flagrant sins of society. We tend to ignore our own sins of pride, selfishness, gossip, and the like. So, effectively, no one sins anymore. The reason is that we have lost sight of the biblical meaning of sin.

The Greek word for sin means "missing the mark," or a miscalculation, but that definition fails to convey to us today the seriousness of our sin. How, then, can we begin to understand how God views our sin?

Four words from Scripture, one from the New Testament and three from the Old Testament, have helped me confront the seriousness of my sin, even the more subtle sins of the heart.

Lawlessness (see 1 John 3:4). John said that sin is lawlessness —

that is, a complete disregard for the law of God. Suppose that over the course of years of driving, you receive two tickets for speeding. No one would consider you a lawless person. But suppose you consistently receive speeding tickets until you lose your driver's license and then continue to drive, even without a license, and you continue to violate the speed-limit laws? Then you could be described as lawless because you have demonstrated a complete disregard for the traffic laws of the state.

Probably not one of us could identify with a person who consistently and deliberately violates the ordinary traffic laws of the state, yet we all consistently and deliberately violate the moral law of God. We consistently display our pride and selfishness; our impatience, anger, and resentment; and our sinful use of the tongue. We consistently fail to display the fruit of the Spirit: love, joy, peace, patience, kindness, goodness, faithfulness, gentleness, self-control (see Galatians 5:22-23). And in that sense, we are all guilty of lawlessness.

Transgression (see Leviticus 16:21 and many other Old Testament references). The word *transgression* means rebellion against authority, in this case God's authority. This is where it is helpful to see the holiness of God as speaking of His transcendent majesty, His supreme and authoritative rule. When we sin we rebel against that authority. Sin is a willful rebellion against the supreme authority of the universe, a deliberate flouting of His moral law.

Despising (see 2 Samuel 12:9-10). *Despise* is the word the prophet Nathan used when he confronted King David about his sins of adultery with Bathsheba and then having her husband, Uriah, killed in battle. David despised God's law, deliberately breaking the commandments forbidding adultery and murder.

But more than that, God, speaking through Nathan the prophet, said, "You have despised me" (2 Samuel 12:10). To despise God's law is to despise Him, as His law is not only an expression of His will but also a reflection of His own moral character. To despise God's law is to effectively say, "I don't care what You say. I will do as I please. I will gossip about or slander someone despite the fact You have said that I am to 'speak evil of no one' [Titus 3:2]." More than that, it is also to say in effect, "God, in my continued sinfulness, I don't want to be like You." We do not consciously say this to God, but, to use an old saying, our actions speak louder than our words.

Defiance (see Numbers 15:30). That passage speaks of the person "who does anything with a high hand." A high hand is an expression of *defiance* — willful rebellion, a deliberate challenge to authority (in our case, a deliberate challenge of God's authority). This might seem like an overstatement because we don't see ourselves as deliberately defying God, but that is actually what we do through our sin.

These four words — lawlessness, rebellion, despise, and defiance — have a certain amount of overlap, but taken together in a cumulative fashion, they help us understand to some degree the seriousness of our sin, even those subtle or "respectable" sins that we so easily tolerate in our lives. We may not be guilty of the more flagrant sins of society around us, but neither was Isaiah. Yet when confronted with the infinite holiness of God, he pronounced himself morally unclean — a moral leper, if you please — and we are no better than Isaiah.

SIN NATURE

Sin, however, is more than wrong actions, unkind words, and even evil thoughts we never express. Sin is a perverted principle or moral force in our hearts, our inner beings. Old Testament scholar Alec Motyer said, "It is the inner reality of the deviant nature" or "the pervertedness of human nature, the result of the fall and the ever flowing fount of sin.[1] David referred to this sin nature when he said, "Surely I was sinful at birth, sinful from the time my mother conceived me" (Psalm 51:5, N I V). Before he was even born, David was a sinner because of the sin nature he had inherited from Adam. This is true of all of us. This is what Paul called the "flesh" (NIV: "sinful nature") in Galatians 5:17.

The author of Hebrews wrote of "sin which clings so closely" (12:1). The King James Version of the Bible renders it "the sin which doth so easily beset us." As a result, for years people have referred to their "besetting sins" — that is, sins to which they are particularly vulnerable. While it is true that most of us have some persistent sins we struggle with (such as anger, gossip, or lust), that does not seem to be what the writer has in mind. Rather, as New Testament scholar F. F. Bruce wrote, "Our author is not referring so much to some specific sin, but sin itself."[2]

What I want us to see, however, is that the author wrote of sin that *clings so closely*. Sin clings to us as tightly as plastic wrap clings to glass. It is not that we walk through life generally unscathed by sin, but occasionally it reaches out and grabs us — no, it clings to us all the time. And why is this so? It is because we still have the flesh, the sin nature, residing *in* us. It clings *to* us because it still resides *in* us. Even though we have been given a renewed heart (see Ezekiel 36:26-27), the sin nature still resides within us and taints every aspect of our being.

Some of us have been Christians for years and have more or less sought to live a life of obedience. Because of that, we may have lost sight of the fact that we are still practicing sinners desperately in need of God's mercy every day. The fact is, our best works are stained with impure (that is, mixed) motives and imperfect performance. We never achieve loving God with all our hearts and our neighbor as ourselves. As Augustine is quoted as saying, "Our best works are but 'splendid vices' in the sense they are less than the perfection God requires."

WHY?

Why this emphasis on the seriousness of sin? Two reasons. First, most Christians do not take their own sin seriously. The self-esteem, "feel good about yourself" movement has so infected the church that it is unfashionable to consider ourselves sinners. There is a popular expression, "We are no longer sinners. We are saints who sin." That statement may be true as far as our basic identity in Christ is concerned. We have indeed been delivered from the dominion of sin, but we are still practicing sinners every day in thought, word, and deed. We don't take our sin seriously because we compare ourselves with others and we tend to maximize their sins and minimize our own. We consider ourselves better than most people. This is why we must always see ourselves not in comparison with those around us but in light of the infinite holiness of God.

This is a book about being transformed into the image of Jesus. It is a book about being holy as God is holy. It is a book about spiritual growth, if you please. But here is a basic truth: We will not grow unless we see our need to grow, we will not pursue holiness unless we see how much we are still unholy, and we will not see our unholiness unless we look at the holiness of God instead of what we perceive to be the unholiness of our neighbor. This is why we must face up to the sinfulness of our own sin. Our sins are not mere "mistakes"; no, they are acts of lawlessness, of rebellion, of despising God and His law. (And here, as I write this, I have to stop and confess to God the sinfulness of my own sin.)

The second reason for dwelling on the seriousness of sin is to cause us to realize our need of the gospel and our need of embracing it every day. It is against the dark backdrop of our sinfulness that the beauty of the gospel shines so brilliantly. Nothing prepares a person to understand and embrace the gospel so much as a personal awareness and conviction of one's own sin. Nineteenth-century Scottish theologian James Buchanan wrote,

> The best preparation for the study of [the gospel] is neither great intellectual ability nor much scholastic learning but a conscience impressed with a sense of our actual condition as sinners in the sight of God. A deep conviction of sin is the one thing needful in such an inquiry, a conviction of the fact of sin, as an awful reality in our own personal experience of the power of sin as an inveterate evil cleaving to us continually, and having its roots deep in the inner-most recesses of our hearts.[3]

You might ask, "What does the gospel have to do with our spiritual transformation? Isn't spiritual transformation just a matter of growing in obedience to the Word of God?" In reality, the gospel has everything to do with our spiritual transformation.

First, the gospel keeps us from discouragement as we see how continually and how far short we come in obedience. All who seek to seriously pursue holiness will invariably become aware of sins they never knew they had. And if we do not believe that our sins are forgiven through the death of Christ, we can easily despair of ever becoming more holy.

Second, the gospel keeps us from self-righteousness because the gospel is only for sinners. Embracing the gospel every day forces me to acknowledge I am still a sinner in need of the mercy of God. It keeps me from lapsing into a performance-based rela-tionship with God because I know that my performance is never good enough.

Third, as we will see in chapter 6, the gospel is the great moti-vator for pursuing spiritual transformation. I will not develop this point now because I will do so extensively in that chapter.

REPENTANCE

As we stress the sinfulness of our sin, we need to consider the place of repentance in the life of a believer. We rightfully stress the importance of repentance in a person's coming to Christ for salvation. People do need to turn from whatever might keep them from trusting Christ alone for salvation. This might be particular sins they need to turn from. Oftentimes it is a person's dependence on their own good deeds that they think will get them to heaven.

However, repentance is not to be a one-time event in coming to Christ but rather a continual act based on a growing awareness of and conviction of sin in our daily lives. This type of a believer's repentance is first of all attitudinal. It should be marked by contrition and a deep realization that our sin, however it may affect other people, is really against God. It is the attitude of David, who, in his own prayer of repentance, said, "Against you, you only, have I sinned and done what is evil in your sight" (Psalm 51:4).

The continually repentant Christian will be poor in spirit and will mourn over his or her sin as being against an infinitely holy God (see Matthew 5:3-4). This person will find solace in the promise that God will not despise a broken and contrite heart (see Psalm 51:17). We hear a lot about the brokenness of people today, but we need to distinguish between our moral brokenness and circumstantial brokenness. Moral brokenness occurs as a result of deep conviction of our own sin, as David displayed in his penitential prayer in Psalm 51.

Circumstantial brokenness often occurs as the result of some other person's (or persons') sin against us. It might be the result of a dysfunctional family situation or childhood physical or sexual abuse or even the devastating actions of someone toward us as adults. It might be circumstances beyond our control, such as a major financial reversal or the death of a loved one. My perception of our present Christian culture is that most people, when they speak of their brokenness, have circumstantial brokenness in mind. Few seem to experience moral brokenness. Conviction of sins now and then, yes, but not the deep poverty of spirit and mourning over sin that Jesus referred to in Matthew 5:3-4 and David expressed in Psalm 51.

I don't mean to belittle the seriousness of circumstantial brokenness and the deep pain it can cause. I also realize that circumstantial brokenness is one of the major instruments the Holy Spirit uses in transforming us into the image of Christ (see chapter 12). But our focus in this chapter is on our own sin — our own moral brokenness, not the sins of other people against us.

So repentance begins with an attitude of brokenness over our sin. But true repentance will be followed by an earnest desire and a sincere effort to put away the sin we are repenting of — to put on the Christlike virtues that we see missing in our lives. These efforts often seem to be characterized by failure as much as by success. But the frequent failures should bring us back to a broken and contrite heart that mourns over our sin. Brokenness, contrition, and repentance are all marks of a growing Christian, a person who is experiencing the work of the Spirit in being transformed gradually more into the image of God's Son.

It may seem as if I am overly belaboring the sinfulness of our sin, but I am convinced that I have not painted the picture nearly as dark as it is to our infinitely holy God. Furthermore, we will not see our continual need of the gospel if we do not see our continual sinfulness. I believe that we do not truly appreciate the gospel until we become desperate for it. But the good news of the gospel is that Christ died to pay the penalty of our sins. All of them. The "big" sins and "little" sins, the sins we are painfully conscious of, and the sins we are not even aware of. As Horatio Spafford said so well in his wonderful hymn "It Is Well with My Soul," "My sin not in part, but the whole, is nailed to the cross and I bare it no more, praise the Lord, praise the Lord, O my soul." That is the gospel, dear friend, and to that gospel we will turn in the next chapter.

FOR GROUP DISCUSSION

1. Have you ever had anything like a "nano experience" of the holiness of God? If so, describe it. If not, how can you seek to have one?

2. How does our perception of our sinfulness change when we see it in the light of God's holiness instead of by comparing ourselves with others?

3. What is meant by "We do not truly appreciate the gospel until we become desperate for it"? Do you agree? Why or why not?

CHAPTER FOUR

The Great Exchange

*One of the seraphim flew to me, having in his hand a burning coal
that he had taken with tongs from the altar. And he touched
my mouth and said: "Behold, this has touched your lips;
your guilt is taken away, and your sin atoned for."*

ISAIAH 6:6-7

In the previous chapter, we left Isaiah totally undone, seeing
himself as a moral leper in the presence of an infinitely holy
God. If we left Isaiah there, there would be no hope for him or for
us either. But God does not leave Isaiah in his hopeless condition.
Instead, He sends one of the seraphim to proclaim the gospel to
him: "Your guilt is taken away, and your sin atoned for" (6:7).

THE GOSPEL TO ISAIAH

God does not say to Isaiah, "I'm sorry you feel so bad about yourself. You really are a good person." Rather, He addresses Isaiah's
real condition: his guilt and his sin. The good news of the gospel is
not that we are not so bad; the good news is that God, through
Christ, has dealt with our badness. How has He done this? How
could God tell Isaiah that his guilt is taken away? Can God just
sweep Isaiah's sin (and ours) under some cosmic rug?

No. God's justice must be satisfied. The least sin in our eyes is rebellion against God's sovereign authority and must be justly punished. God cannot, in view of the infinite perfection of all His attributes, exalt one at the expense of another, and so God cannot exalt His mercy at the expense of His justice; justice must be satisfied.

Therefore, on what basis did God forgive Isaiah's sin? He did it on the same basis for which He forgives our sin: the death of Jesus Christ, which would occur, as we reckon time, about seven hundred years later, but in God's eternal timelessness, before the foundation of the world. The Bible is quite clear that "without the shedding of blood there is no forgiveness of sins" (Hebrews 9:22). And John wrote in Revelation 1:5, "To him who loves us and has freed us from our sins by his blood." So Isaiah's guilt was taken away and his sin atoned for because Jesus died and shed His blood for Isaiah as well as for you and me. God's justice and God's mercy met at the cross, and both are duly magnified.

The seraphim touched Isaiah's mouth with the burning coal from the altar. It was Isaiah's unclean lips that made him so painfully aware of his sin, so it is his lips that are cleansed with the burning coal. The gospel addresses all of our sin, but there are times when we need it to address specific sins in our lives. There are times when we are so painfully conscious of some sin that we need to hear the words of Colossians 2:13, "He forgave us all our sins" (NIV), addressed to that specific sin.

FORGIVENESS AND RIGHTEOUSNESS

But as important as is the forgiveness of our sins — and believe me, it is very important — there is more to the gospel than forgiveness. There is also the righteousness of Christ, which is credited to all who trust in Him, plus all the additional blessings that flow out of the gospel. And here I should say that I use the word *gospel*, which actually means "good news," as a shorthand expression for all that Christ accomplished for us in His sinless life and His death on the cross. So at this point, we want to take a good look at the gospel, and there is no better Scripture to help us do that than 2 Corinthians 5:21: "For our sake he made him to be sin who knew no sin, so that in him we might become the righteousness of God."

The late New Testament commentator Philip Hughes wrote concerning this verse, "There is no sentence more profound in the whole of Scripture; for this verse embraces the whole ground of the sinner's reconciliation to God."[1] And nineteenth-century theologian Charles Hodge wrote, "There is probably no passage in the Scriptures in which the doctrine of justification is more concisely or clearly stated."[2]

Speaking personally, 2 Corinthians 5:21 is my all-time favorite verse. If in old age my memory begins to fail, I pray that I can at least remember this verse.

OUR CONDITION

As we look at this verse, we see three pronouns: *our* (referring to us), *he* (that is, God the Father), and *him* (that is, Christ Jesus). For our sake, God did something to His Son. What is the condition of those of us for whom God did something? In Romans 5:6-10, Paul described us as weak (or helpless), ungodly, sinners, and enemies of God. Though Adam was created in the image of God, through his rebellion in the garden, that image was seriously defaced and the whole human race became enemies of God, objects of His wrath (see Ephesians 2:3).

What is the solution? Paul continued in Ephesians 2:4-6,

But God, being rich in mercy, because of the great love with which he loved us, even when we were dead in our trespasses, made us alive together with Christ — by grace you have been saved — and raised us up with him and seated us with him in the heavenly places in Christ Jesus.

Note the words Paul used: *rich in mercy, great love, grace.* God in His great love, expressed through His mercy and grace, provided the solution by sending His own Son to live and die in our place. As John 3:16 says, "God so loved the world, that he gave his only Son." The "world" in this instance stands for the sum total of humanity living in a state of rebellion against Him. There is nothing in us to commend us to God. He acted out of His own self-generated love and mercy toward sinful, rebellious beings.

Peter said in 2 Peter 2:4 that God did not spare angels when they sinned but cast them into hell to await the final judgment. God could have done the same with the human race and been perfectly just. He could have allowed each of us to be born, to live out a miserable existence in a sin-cursed world, and then die and be cast into hell. Instead, God, out of His own love and mercy, did something for us. God did something to His Son for our sake.

THE SINLESSNESS OF CHRIST

But before we look at what God did to His Son, let's look at what Paul said about Him. Paul said, "[He] knew no sin." Jesus was not born with a sinful nature as we are. He had no internal guerilla warfare between the flesh and the Spirit as we have. He had no ulterior or self-seeking motives. He never struggled with internal temptation. He knew no sin.

The writer of Hebrews said that Jesus was tempted in every respect as we are but without sin (see 4:15). He had no internal warfare, but He was confronted with every kind of external temptation. Jesus did not grow up in a morally sterile environment. He had four half brothers and several sisters (see Matthew 13:55-56). Though they were all probably well-taught Jewish children, they all had a sinful nature, as we have. There were undoubtedly frequent external temptations to sin as Jesus interacted with His brothers and sisters, but He never sinned. As a teenager and young adult, He undoubtedly was confronted with many temptations peculiar to that age, but He never gave in to them. At the beginning of His public ministry at about thirty years of age, He was severely tempted by the Devil (see Matthew 4:1-11) but successfully resisted those temptations. In every respect, He was without sin.

The apostle Peter testified that in the face of reviling and suffering, "he committed no sin" (1 Peter 2:22-23). The apostle John wrote that "in him there is no sin" (1 John 3:5). Thus we see that the four major writers of the New Testament letters — Paul, Peter, John, and the writer of Hebrews — all testify to the sinlessness of Jesus.

But an even greater testimony comes from the mouth of Jesus Himself. John 8:12-59 records an increasingly hostile dialogue Jesus had with a group of Jews. At one point, Jesus said to them, "You are of your father the devil" (verse 44), and at the end of the confrontation, the Jews picked up stones to throw at Him (see verse 59). In the course of that hostile dialogue, Jesus said of Himself, "I always do the things that are pleasing to [the Father]" (verse 29). And again, after He had said to them, "You are of your father the devil," He dared to ask them, "Which one of you convicts me of sin?" (verse 46). He dared to ask the question because He was confident of the answer. He was without sin. Throughout His entire lifetime, Jesus perfectly and completely obeyed all the law of God. To use His own words in Matthew 5:18, He obeyed every iota and dot (or, as many of us are more familiar with from King James, every jot and tittle) of the law.

Why this emphasis on the sinlessness of Jesus? There are two reasons. First, in order to die for our sins, He had to be sinless Himself. He had to be morally without blemish or spot (see Hebrews 9:14; 1 Peter 1:19). Second, as we will see more as we continue through 2 Corinthians 5:21, He had to compile a record of perfect righteousness that could be transferred to us. But for now, the next question is what did God the Father do to His sinless Son?

GOD MADE HIM TO BE SIN

The answer is shocking. He made Him to be sin. This seemingly strange expression of Paul is his way of saying that Jesus was made to be the very embodiment of sin. He was made to be all that which is abominable and hateful to God — all that which is the object of His holy and just wrath. As our substitute, He was made to be the embodiment of all our rebellion, all our lawlessness, all of our despising of God and His law, all of our "big" sins and "little" sins, even all the sins of which we are not aware because of the moral "blind spots" so many of us have. Yes, Jesus was made to be all of that. For our sake, He was made to be sin.

Peter expressed it a little differently. He said, "He himself bore our sins in his body on the tree [that is, the cross]" (1 Peter 2:24). So what happened as God made Jesus to be sin, or to bear our sin? God poured out His just and holy wrath on His own Son, whom He had made to be the very embodiment of sin. The most vivid description of God's action is in Isaiah 53. Consider certain phrases I have extracted from that beautiful chapter:

- He was *smitten* by God. (verse 4)
- He was *wounded* for our transgressions. (verse 5)
- He was *crushed* for our iniquities. (verse 5)
- He was *stricken* for our transgressions. (verse 8)
- It was the will of the Lord to *crush* him. (verse 10)

Note the italicized words. They speak of not just the physical agony Jesus suffered, which was horrible beyond our imagination, but more important the spiritual agony He endured as He drank the cup of the wrath of God. And bear in mind it was for our sake that God made Him to bear that agony.

THE RIGHTEOUSNESS OF GOD

The remainder of 2 Corinthians 5:21 says, "In him we might be made the righteousness of God." Again this is another difficult phrase to understand, but it will help if we seek to answer three questions:

1. What is the righteousness of God in this verse?
2. How do we become the righteousness of God?
3. What is the meaning of "in him"?

First, what is the righteousness of God to which Paul was referring? I believe the clearest answer is to be found in Philippians 3:9, which occurs in Paul's testimony of how he turned decisively from a righteousness of his own through obedience to God's law to the righteousness from God that depends on faith. In Paul's letters, Christ Jesus is always the object of faith, so the righteousness that is from God can be only the righteousness of Christ Himself lived out in His thirty-three years of earthly existence. So in effect Paul was saying, "I want to be found in Christ, not having a righteousness of my own that comes from my personal obedience to the law but that which comes through faith in Christ and His perfect righteousness."

How then do we become the righteousness of God? The answer is that when by faith we trust in Jesus, God credits His perfect obedience, or His perfect righteousness, to us. We can see now the second necessity for Christ's sinlessness or, to state it in the language of 2 Corinthians 5:21, His righteousness. Just as God made Christ to be sin and charged the guilt of our sin to Him, so He credits the righteousness of Christ to those who have faith in Him. This is why 2 Corinthians 5:21 is so often called the Great Exchange. God exchanges our sin for Christ's righteousness.

UNION WITH CHRIST

This brings us to the third question, what is the meaning of the two-word phrase "in Him"? This expression — "in Him," or "in Christ," or "in the Lord" — together with a similar expression — "with Christ," or "with Him" — occurs more than 150 times in Paul's letters. These expressions are Paul's way of speaking of our union with Christ. There are basically two aspects of this union. The first is our representative union, wherein Christ acted as our representative in both His sinless life and sin-bearing death. The second is what we may call the living union, wherein Christ lives within us by His Holy Spirit and empowers us to live the Christian life.

But it is the representative union with Christ that is in view in Paul's use of "in him" in 2 Corinthians 5:21. To understand this phrase, "representative union," we must go to Romans 5:12-21, where Paul taught us that Adam was appointed by God to represent the entire human race. In a sense, we were all "in Adam," just as we are "in Christ." Therefore, when Adam sinned, we all sinned, and the guilt and consequences of his sin fall upon all humanity. That is why we are all born spiritually dead, subject to the domain of Satan, and by nature children of God's wrath (see Ephesians 2:1-3).

But Paul drew an analogy and by contrast taught us that just as Adam was the representative head of all humanity, so Christ is the representative head of all who trust in Him as Savior. So just as we must say, "When Adam sinned, I sinned," we may also say, "When Christ died on the cross, I died on the cross." In fact, this is what Paul essentially said when he wrote, "I have been crucified with Christ" (Galatians 2:20). Furthermore, we may also say, "When Christ lived a perfect, sinless life, I lived a perfect, sinless life." I realize that this last statement is breathtaking, but that is what Paul was saying in his words, "In him we might become the righteousness of God."

This representative union with Christ is key to understanding the gospel. In fact, more than that, it is what makes Christ's life and death effective for us. If Christ did not legally represent us, all that He did would be of no avail to us.

The living union is best represented by the metaphor of the vine and the branches that Jesus used in John 15:1-6. Just as the branches derive their life and nourishment from the vine, so we derive our spiritual life and nourishment from Christ through this living union. We will address this union more in chapter 8. Meanwhile, keep in mind that the representative and the living union are only two expressions of the one union. In the one expression, we stand righteous before God. In the other, we experience the life and power of Christ in our daily lives.

JUSTIFICATION

The result of God's Great Exchange of charging our sin to Christ and crediting His righteousness to us is justification. Justification means that in our standing before God, we are righteous in His sight. We are obviously not righteous in our daily experience any more than Christ was sinful in His daily experience. But when by faith we trust in Him, God regards us as righteous because He has credited to us the righteousness of Christ.

There is an old play on the word *justified*, that it means "just as if I'd never sinned." That expression speaks to the forgiveness of our sins. When God charges our sins to Christ, they are no longer ours. He has removed them from us as far as the east is from the west (see Psalm 103:12). He remembers them no more (see Hebrews 8:12). The penalty has been paid. God's justice is satisfied. His judicial wrath has been fully exhausted on His Son. Truly we stand before Him just as if we'd never sinned!

But there is another play on the word *justification*, that it also means "just as if I had always obeyed." That is also a glorious truth that is based on the perfect obedience of Christ — the obedience that, as we have already seen, was lived out over thirty-three years of real human life in a real world.

In chapter 2, we saw that the holiness of God includes His infinite moral purity. Consider this: Jesus in His humanity was just as holy as God sitting on His throne. There was not one iota of difference. And what Jesus was in His life, we are in our standing before God because Jesus was our representative in both His life and death. So as far as our standing before God is concerned, when He lived a perfect life, *we* lived a perfect life. When He died on the cross, *we* died on the cross. All that Jesus did in both His sinless life and sin-bearing death, He did as our representative and substitute.

That's why the apostle Paul could write, "As by the one man's disobedience the many were made sinners, so by the one man's obedience the many will be made righteous" (Romans 5:19). Obviously, based on the overall teaching of the New Testament, the "many" in those two comparisons are not equal in extent. The first many who were made sinners refers to the entire human race (except, of course, Jesus). The second many refers to all who are united to Christ by faith. Paul is not teaching a universal salvation of all humankind.

So because of God's Great Exchange, all who trust in Christ as Savior stand before God "just as if we'd never sinned" and "just as if we had always obeyed." Once after I had spoken on the Great Exchange, a man said to me, "I still don't understand the difference." He had already told me he was a self-employed landscape contractor, so I said to him, "Suppose you have been working on a job all day and you come home sweaty and dirty and your clothes all grimy. What do you need to do before you sit down to dinner?"

He replied, "I need to take a shower and put on clean clothes."

"How about just putting on clean clothes without taking a shower?"

"No, I would never do that," he replied.

"Then how about taking a shower and putting your grimy work clothes back on?"

"No, I wouldn't do that either."

"So you need to both take a shower and put on clean clothes?"

"Yes," he replied, "that's what I need to do."

I said, "That's what God does to you. He washes you clean in the blood of His Son and clothes you in His perfect righteousness." He smiled and said, "I get it."

The question is, do we "get it"? Do we really believe that every day our standing before God is based entirely, as the old hymn puts it, on "Jesus' blood and righteousness"? Our natural drift is toward a performance-based relationship with God. So if my concept of sin consists of only the more flagrant sins of society of which I am not guilty, I will tend toward a confident self-righteousness epitomized by the Pharisee who prayed in the temple, "God, I thank you that I am not like other men" (Luke 18:11). On the other hand, those who have a tender conscience and see so much of their own "respectable" sins will often live under a continual sense of God's displeasure.

What is the solution to a performance-based relationship with God that tends toward either self-righteousness or a continual sense of guilt? It is a daily living in the reality of the Great Exchange. It is a daily believing that however vile my sins are in my eyes, God has said, "Though your sins are like scarlet, they shall be as white as snow" (Isaiah 1:18). It is believing that in every instance where I have failed to obey, Jesus has already obeyed in my place (see Philippians 3:9). In short, it is a daily embracing of the gospel, looking outside of myself to Jesus and His shed blood and righteousness. And we will see what that looks like in the next chapter.

FOR GROUP DISCUSSION

1. What is meant by "God cannot exalt His *mercy* at the expense of His justice; justice must be satisfied." Do you agree? Why or why not?

2. Exactly what is exchanged in "the Great Exchange"? What is required from us in order to participate in this exchange?

3. If by authentic faith we are "in Christ" and Jesus is truly our representative, how does God see us from that point in time forward? What about the sin we commit next week?

CHAPTER FIVE

A Daily Embracing of the Gospel

*We ourselves are Jews by birth and not Gentile sinners; yet we
know that a person is not justified by works of the law but through
faith in Jesus Christ, so we also have believed in Christ Jesus, in
order to be justified by faith in Christ and not by works of the law,
because by works of the law no one will be justified.*

GALATIANS 2:15-16

As we see in the text above, the apostle Paul was very emphatic
that a person is not justified by works of the law but through
faith in Jesus Christ. He was so emphatic that he was obviously
redundant, effectively saying the same thing three times in one
long sentence. Why was Paul so troubled? Because the Galatian
believers were in danger of adding circumcision and law keeping
to faith in Jesus Christ for their salvation.

So Paul continued to hammer away at this false teaching. In
fact, just four paragraphs later he wrote, "All who rely on works of
the law are under a curse; for it is written, 'Cursed be everyone
who does not abide by all things written in the Book of the Law,
and do them'" (Galatians 3:10). Effectively, Paul was saying, "So
you want to be saved by keeping the law, do you? Let me tell you
what that would look like. It means absolute perfect obedience to

all the law of God." Note the word *all*. That means *all* without exception. To use an academic analogy, that means getting a 99 on your final exam equals failing the course. Nothing less than 100 percent correct is a passing grade.

And what is the law of God? It is all the moral will of God throughout Scripture in both the Old and New Testaments. But Jesus summed it all up for us when He said,

> You shall love the Lord your God with all your heart and with all your soul and with all your mind. This is the great and first commandment. And a second is like it: You shall love your neighbor as yourself. On these two commandments depend all the Law and the Prophets. (Matthew 22:37-40)

The reality is that no one (except Christ) has ever come close to obeying either of those commandments. No one has ever loved God with all his being. No one has ever fully loved his neighbor as himself. So where would that leave the Galatians, who were in danger of adding law keeping to faith in Christ? Persistence in it would leave them under the curse of God. Instead of law keeping being even partially a means of salvation, it would actually leave them under a curse.

That is why Paul was so emphatic that justification is entirely by faith in Christ alone. Dependence on one's law keeping and faith in Christ are mutually exclusive. In fact, faith involves a total renunciation of dependence on one's good works and instead total reliance on Jesus Christ and His righteousness.

HOW ABOUT US?

Now, it is likely that most readers of this book will understand and agree with in principle (if not in every detail) what I have written thus far. And indeed you may be thinking, *What's the big deal? This is elementary; this is "Gospel 101," but what's the relevance to me? I am relying on Christ alone for my salvation. I am not in danger of adding law keeping or good works to my faith in Christ as were the Galatians.*

The relevance of Paul's warning to the Galatians is this: We all, having trusted in Christ alone for our salvation, have a tendency to revert to a performance-based relationship with God. We know we are saved by faith in Christ alone, but we assume we earn God's acceptance and blessings in our daily lives by our performance.

Some thirty years ago, Professor Richard Lovelace of Gordon-Conwell Seminary wrote,

> Only a fraction of the present body of professing Christians are solidly appropriating the justifying work of Christ in their lives. Many have so light an apprehension of God's holiness and of the extent and guilt of their sin that consciously they see little need for justification, although below the surface of their lives they are deeply guilt-ridden and insecure. Many others have a theoretical commitment to this doctrine, but in their day-to-day existence they rely on their sanctification for justification, drawing their assurance of acceptance with God from their sincerity, their past experience of conversion, their recent religious performance or the relative infrequency of their conscious, willful disobedience.[1]

What is the solution? We must learn to live as Paul lived. In Galatians 2:20, he wrote, "The life I now live in the flesh I live by faith in the Son of God, who loved me and gave himself for me." In the context of verses 15-21, Paul was talking about justification and is speaking in the present tense: "the life I *now* live." Elsewhere, in Romans 5:1, he spoke of justification as a point-in-time past experience: "Since we have been [past tense] justified by faith, we have peace with God through our Lord

Jesus Christ." If justification, then, is a past experience, why does Paul in Galatians 2:20 write of it in the present tense? The answer is that for Paul, justification was not only a past experience but *also a present reality*. Every day Paul looked outside of himself and his performance to the perfect righteousness of Christ for his acceptance with God the Father.

If we want to enjoy the benefits of the gospel in our daily lives, we must learn to live like Paul. We must learn to look outside of ourselves and our performance, whether good or bad, and see ourselves standing before God justified — cleansed from our sins through the shed blood of Christ and clothed in the perfect righteousness of Christ.

Sadly, this great truth of the gospel seems to be so little understood and even less applied by the vast majority of believers. Again, Professor Lovelace wrote,

> Few [Christians] know enough to start each day with a thoroughgoing stand upon Luther's platform: you are accepted, looking outward in faith and claiming the wholly [external] righteousness of Christ, as the only ground of acceptance, relaxing in that quality of trust which will produce increasing sanctification [or transformation] as faith is active in love and gratitude.[2]

This emphasis on the need of daily embracing the gospel and living in the present reality of our justification is not new and novel. We have already seen Professor Lovelace's comments written in 1979. But let's go back further than that. B. B. Warfield was a noted theologian who taught at Princeton Theological Seminary in the late nineteenth and early twentieth centuries. Sometime during that period, he wrote the following:

> There is nothing in us or done by us at any stage of our earthly development because of which we are acceptable

to God. We must always be accepted for Christ's sake or we cannot ever be accepted at all. This is not true of us only "when we believe," it is just as true after we have believed. It will continue to be true as long as we live. Our need of Christ does not cease with our believing nor does the nature of our relation to Him or to God through Him ever alter no matter what our attainments in Christian graces or our achievements in Christian behavior may be. It is always on His "blood and righteousness" alone that we can rest. There is never anything that we are or have or do that can take His place or that takes a place along with Him. We are always unworthy, and all that we have or do of good is always of pure grace. Though blessed with every spiritual blessing in the heavenlies in Christ, we are still in ourselves just "miserable sinners." "Miserable sinners" saved by grace, to be sure. But "miserable sinners" still deserving in ourselves nothing but everlasting wrath.

We are sinners, and we know ourselves to be sinners lost and helpless in ourselves; but we are saved sinners, and it is our salvation which gives the tone to our life — a tone of joy which swells in exact proportion to the sense we have of our ill-desert. For it is he to whom much is forgiven who loves much and, who loving, rejoices much.

Thus, through every moment of his life, the believer is absolutely dependent on the grace of Christ, and when life is over, he still has nothing to plead but Christ's blood and righteousness.[3]

Much earlier, the Scotsman Robert Haldane (1774–1842), in his classic commentary on the book of Romans, wrote,

To that righteousness is the eye of the believer ever to be directed; on that righteousness must he rest; on that righteousness must he live; on that righteousness must he die; in that righteousness must he appear before the judgment seat; in that righteousness must he stand for ever in the presence of a righteous God.[4]

So the moment you trusted in Christ alone, you were declared righteous by God because He credited to you the perfect righteousness of Christ. You will never be more or less righteous, regardless of your performance. In fact, today you are as righteous in your standing with God as you will be in heaven. This seems astonishing, but it is true.

The question may well be asked, "Does my righteous standing with God because of Christ's righteousness translate into the expectation of daily blessings from Him because of Christ's righteousness?" The answer is an emphatic yes. God does not justify us on one basis and bless us daily on another. All of God's favor to us, whether in the spiritual or temporal realms, comes to us through Christ.

Paul wrote in Ephesians 1:3, "Blessed be the God and Father of our Lord Jesus Christ, who has blessed us in Christ with every spiritual blessing in the heavenly places." Note the phrase "in Christ." Remember, this is Paul's shorthand expression for our representative union with Christ. So all spiritual blessings come to us through Christ.

Again, in Philippians 4:19, Paul wrote, "My God will supply every need of yours according to his riches in glory in Christ Jesus." In the context of Philippians 4:10-19, the "every need" of verse 19 refers to the Philippian believers' temporal needs. In effect, Paul was saying to them, "Just as you have been instruments of God to supply my temporal needs, so God will also supply your temporal needs." But again notice the phrase "in Christ Jesus." It is always "in Christ" — that is, because of Him and through Him — that all of our blessings, both spiritual and temporal, come to us.

We never, of ourselves, earn God's blessings through our good works because even our very best deeds are imperfect in accomplishment and defiled by our remaining sinful corruption. Those good works on which we tend to rely for our expectation of God's blessings actually deserve the curse of God rather than His blessing. But thanks be to God, Christ has redeemed us from the curse of the law by taking our curse upon Himself (see Galatians 3:13) and has instead, through His perfect righteousness, opened the floodgates of God's infinite love and favor toward us, all this "to the praise of his glorious grace, with which he has blessed us in the Beloved" (Ephesians 1:6).

My all-time favorite quote outside the Bible, one to which I return almost daily, is the first few words of the hymn "My Hope Is Built": "My hope is built on nothing less than Jesus' blood and righteousness." For me, that hope is not only for eternal life but for God's favor and blessing on my life today.

EVERY DAY'S WORK

How then do we learn to live daily in the present reality of our justification and the hope of God's blessings on our lives coming to us through Christ? The answer is we must work at it daily. As I stated previously, we have a natural drift toward a performance-based relationship with God. We are like a person in a rowboat trying to row upstream against the current. The instant the rower stops pulling on his or her oars, the boat will start drifting backward with the current. We can never, as the old saying goes, "rest on our oars" in our daily dependence on Christ. Practically speaking, how do we keep plugging along? We go to the Scriptures containing the promises of God regarding the forgiveness of our sins and the imputation (crediting) to us of Christ's perfect righteousness.

The following are Scriptures regarding God's promise of forgiveness of our sins:

As far as the east is from the west, so far does he remove our transgressions from us. (Psalm 103:12)

Come now, let us reason together, says the Lord: though your sins are like scarlet, they shall be as white as snow; though they are red like crimson, they shall become like wool. (Isaiah 1:18)

I, I am he who blots out your transgressions for my own sake, and I will not remember your sins. (Isaiah 43:25)

All we like sheep have gone astray; we have turned — every one — to his own way; and the LORD has laid on him the iniquity of us all. (Isaiah 53:6)

Blessed are those whose lawless deeds are forgiven, and whose sins are covered; blessed is the man against whom the Lord will not count his sin. (Romans 4:7-8)

There is therefore now no condemnation for those who are in Christ Jesus. (Romans 8:1)

Here are some Scriptures regarding reliance on Christ's perfect righteousness:

As by the one man's disobedience the many were made sinners, so by the one man's obedience the many will be made righteous. (Romans 5:19)

Being ignorant of the righteousness of God, and seeking to establish their own, they did not submit to God's righteousness. For Christ is the end of the law for righteousness to everyone who believes. (Romans 10:3-4)

Because of him you are in Christ Jesus, who became to us wisdom from God, righteousness and sanctification and redemption. (1 Corinthians 1:30)

For our sake he made him to be sin who knew no sin, so that in him we might become the righteousness of God. (2 Corinthians 5:21)

Be found in him, not having a righteousness of my own that comes from the law, but that which comes through faith in Christ, the righteousness from God that depends on faith. (Philippians 3:9)

I encourage you to prayerfully (that is, asking the Holy Spirit to guide you) consider each of these Scriptures and select two or three from each category that seem to speak most forcefully to you. Memorize them and begin to use them every day to strengthen your faith in God's Great Exchange. Then every time you find yourself lapsing into a performance-based relationship with God, go back to those verses and ask God to make them experientially real to you.

Already in this chapter, we have looked at the wise words of Richard Lovelace in the late twentieth century, B. B. Warfield in the late nineteenth or early twentieth century, and Robert Haldane in the early nineteenth century. Now I want to go all the way back to the seventeenth century and consider the words of the great Puritan theologian John Owen on the daily appropriation of the gospel. In the following quotations, I am extracting for the sake of brevity from about three pages in his outstanding work *Communion with the Triune God*.

The saints make an actual exchange with the Lord Jesus as to their sins and His righteousness. Of this there are various parts.

They continually keep alive upon their hearts a sense of the guilt and evil of sin; even when they are under some comfortable persuasions of their personal acceptance with God. Sense of pardon takes away the horror and fear, but not a due sense of the guilt of sin. It is the daily exercise of the saints of God, to consider the great provocation that is in sin — their sins. This the saints do: they gather up their sins, lay them in the balance of the law, see and consider their weight and desert....

They hearken to the voice of Christ calling them to him with their burden. "Come unto me, all you that are weary and heavy laden" [Matthew 11:28] — "Come with your burdens; come, you poor soul, with your guilt of sin." Why? What to do? "Why, this is mine," says Christ; "this agreement I made with my Father, that I should come, and take your sins, and bear them away; they were my lot. Give me your burden, give me all your sins. You know not what to do with them; I know how to dispose of them well enough, so that God shall be glorified, and your soul delivered."...

They lay down their sins at the cross of Christ, upon his shoulders. This is faith's great and bold venture upon the grace, faithfulness, and truth of God, to stand by the cross and say, "Ah! He is bruised for my sins, and wounded for my transgressions, and the chastisement of my peace is upon him. He is thus made sin for me. Here I give up my sins to him that is able to bear them, to undergo them. He requires it of my hands, that I should be content that he should undertake for them; and that I heartily consent unto." This is every day's work; I know not how any peace can be maintained with God without it.

Having thus by faith given up their sins to Christ, and seen God laying them all on him, they draw nigh and take from him that righteousness which he has wrought out for them, so fulfilling the whole of that of the apostle, "He was made sin for us that we might be made the righteousness of God in him" (2 Corinthians 5:21). They consider Him tendering himself and his righteousness, to be their righteousness before God; they take it and accept of it, and complete this blessed bartering and exchange of faith.

This exceedingly endears the souls of the saints to him and constrains them to put a due valuation upon him, his love, his righteousness, and grace. When they find, and have the daily use of it, then they do it. Who would not love him? "I have been with the Lord Jesus," may the poor soul say: "I have left my sins, my burdens with him; and he has given me his righteousness, wherewith I am going with boldness to God.[5]

This is a much longer quotation than I would normally include in a book, but I want you to see what John Owen wrote about 350 years ago. A daily embracing of the gospel is not a new idea. In fact, it goes much further back than seventeenth-century John Owen; it goes all the way back to the apostle Paul!

Also, I want to call your attention to John Owen's words: "It is the daily exercise of the saints to consider the great provocation that is in sin" and "This is every day's work: I know not how any peace can be maintained with the God without it." A daily embracing of the gospel is indeed every day's work. That is why we need to preach the gospel to ourselves every day.

OUR RESPONSE

In Romans 5:20, Paul wrote, "Where sin increased, grace abounded all the more." Paul anticipated a possible wrong conclusion could be drawn from his seemingly unguarded statement and sought to deal with it in Romans 6:1-14. In the same way, a wrong conclusion might be drawn from my strong emphasis on the truth that in

Christ our sins are forgiven, we are counted righteous in Him, and all of God's favor and blessings to us come through Him apart from any works on our part.

At the same time, I am aware that some pastors, missionaries, Bible teachers, and staff members of various Christian ministries will be concerned that the emphasis of this chapter will cut the nerve of the intentional pursuit of transformation that we want to see in the lives of those we teach and shepherd. I understand this concern. I trust that in the next chapter, we all can see from the Scriptures that a daily dependence on Christ is the only true and lasting motivation for pursuing spiritual transformation.

FOR GROUP DISCUSSION

1. What is the meaning of the expression "performance-based relationship with God"? What are some subtle ways this type of relationship shows up in your life?
2. In practical terms, what does it look like when we "stand in the present reality" of our justification? What impact will it have on our relationship with God and other people?
3. In practical terms, what does it mean to "preach the gospel to yourself every day"? How does a person do it?

CHAPTER SIX

The Motivation of the Gospel

I heard the voice of the Lord saying, "Whom shall I send, and who will go for us?" Then I said, "Here am I! Send me."

ISAIAH 6:8

I saiah had been totally devastated, morally and spiritually, by his vision of the infinite holiness of God. Then the seraphim had announced the gospel to him: "Your guilt is taken away, and your sin atoned for" (Isaiah 6:7).

Soon he heard the voice of the Lord saying, "Whom shall I send, and who will go for us?" Isaiah responded, "Here am I! Send me" (verse 8). His response is immediate and spontaneous. He said, "Here am I," not "Here I am." The latter denotes location, whereas, "Here am I" means "I am available." He didn't ask any questions, such as, "Go where?" or "Do what?" He, in effect, gave God a blank check for his life. He said, "Here am I. Send me." Why did he respond in this way? It is because Isaiah was so deeply impacted by the gospel that he responded in heartfelt gratitude to God for what He has done for him.

Let's consider the timing of Isaiah's call. Suppose he had heard the call of God before his vision of God's holiness. If our assumption is correct that he was an outwardly righteous, law-observant

Jew, he might well have responded, "Here am I, Lord. I'm qualified to be Your spokesman." He then would likely have gone to his people in an attitude of self-righteousness rather than love and compassion.

Or suppose Isaiah had heard the call of God after he had been totally devastated over his sin but before he had heard the gospel. His response would probably have been, "Not me, Lord. A few minutes ago I would have volunteered, but not now. I am a man of unclean lips. I am totally unqualified to be Your spokesman."

It was only after he had become painfully aware of his sinfulness and had received the assurance that his sins were forgiven that he was in a position to hear the call of God and respond so immediately out of deep heartfelt gratitude.

Let me enlarge on the word *gratitude*. You may lend me your pen for a moment to sign my name, and as I return it, I say, "Thank you." That's a very basic level of gratitude — actually, a common courtesy. But if you rescue my child from a burning building and I say, "I can never thank you enough," that's a significantly higher level of gratitude. Now take the occasion of our gratitude to the highest possible level: Christ's rescuing us from God's eternal curse by becoming a curse in our place (see Galatians 3:13) and you have Isaiah's gratitude. It is this level of gratitude that will motivate us to obey Christ as Lord and serve Him as Master.

THE SINFUL WOMAN

Isaiah was not the only person in the Bible who demonstrated the sequence of "guilt, gospel, and gratitude" in action. We see it also in the beautiful story of the sinful woman who anointed the feet of Jesus, as recounted by Luke in Luke 7:36-50. The late radio commentator Paul Harvey, in his daily news broadcast, often used his famous line "And now for the rest of the story." The only way this story in Luke 7 makes sense is to assume that Luke gives us the rest of the story. What then is the beginning?

Luke described this woman as a "sinner." He did not tell us the nature of her sin. She may or may not have been an immoral woman, but she did have a bad reputation in the city. Simon the Pharisee was scandalized that Jesus would allow her to touch Him because he knew that she was a "sinner" (verse 39).

The beginning of the story, then, is that this sinful woman had had a prior encounter with Jesus, possibly not long before the story in Luke 7. She, like Isaiah, had become painfully aware of her sin and, again like Isaiah, had received from Jesus the assurance that her sins were forgiven. Picking up the story with Luke's account, Jesus was invited to eat at the house of Simon, a Pharisee. The sinful woman learned of this and went to Simon's house with an alabaster flask of ointment to anoint the feet of Jesus.

According to the custom of the day, it was not unusual for uninvited guests to come into the room where a dinner was being held. They would take a place around the perimeter of the room and listen in on the table conversation. What made the action of the sinful woman unusual was that she, a known sinner with a bad reputation, would dare enter the home of a Pharisee, a group well known for their strict outward observance of the law and also known for their self-righteous attitude toward others. (See Luke's account of the Pharisee and the tax collector praying in the temple, Luke 18:9-14, for a good example.)

Not only does the woman dare enter Simon's home, she does not take a place around the edge of the room; she goes straight to Jesus with the intent of anointing His feet. As she stands behind Him at His feet, she begins to weep — not just a few tears but profusely, so that His feet were wet with her tears. To appreciate her next act, it is helpful to observe that because of Simon's total lack of extending the customary courtesies to Jesus, His feet had not been washed (see verse 44). So when Luke told us that the woman wiped Jesus' feet with her hair, that act was more than simply drying them.

She was actually cleansing them with the hair of her head. Then she kissed His feet and anointed them with the ointment.

Simon was appalled that Jesus would allow this sinful woman with a known reputation to touch Him. Jesus, knowing Simon's thoughts, told him the parable of a moneylender who had two debtors. One owed five hundred denarii and the other fifty. When they could not pay, he cancelled the debt of both. Then Jesus asked Simon who of them would love him more. Simon responded, "The one, I suppose, for whom he cancelled the larger debt." Jesus said to Simon, "You have judged rightly."

Jesus then compared the rather egregious lack of even common courtesy displayed by Simon with the lavish display of affection shown by the sinful woman. His conclusion in verse 47, "Therefore I tell you, her sins, which are many, are forgiven — for she loved much," seems confusing because the statement, taken out of context, seems to mean that she was forgiven because she loved much. This obviously cannot be Jesus' meaning, because it is the very opposite of the point of the moneylender parable. Additionally, it flies in the face of the entire New Testament principle that our love to Christ can only be a response to His love for us.

Rather, Jesus was saying that the woman's lavish display of love to Him was proof that she had already experienced deep down in her soul the reality of His forgiveness. Why then did Jesus say to her at that time, "Your sins are forgiven," if she had already been forgiven?

Remember, this woman was a known sinner in the town. She had a bad reputation, so Jesus' words of forgiveness had a twofold audience in mind. First, Simon and his other guests needed to hear Jesus say that He had the authority to forgive sins, something the Pharisees vehemently questioned (see, for example, Luke 5:17-26). But Jesus' words were also for the woman's benefit through a public declaration that she was forgiven; that her sinful past was made clean; that though her sins were like scarlet, they were made as white as snow (see Isaiah 1:18). Of course, Jesus could say this only in view of the yet-to-be shedding of His own blood that would provide the basis of her forgiveness (see Hebrews 9:22; Revelation 7:14).

CONTRAST AND SIMILARITY

A comparison of the experiences of Isaiah and the sinful woman is a study in both contrast and similarity. By way of contrast, the backgrounds of the two are poles apart. Isaiah was a highly regarded member of the Jewish upper class — a member of the elite of society and presumably a righteous law-observing Jew. The sinful woman, if not a known woman of immorality, certainly had a bad reputation in the city, very likely an outcast from the respectable part of society. In fact, Jesus Himself referred to "her sins, which are many" (Luke 7:47). The contrast could hardly be greater. But their experiences are amazingly similar. Both had an encounter with God. Isaiah saw Him sitting on His throne in His infinite holiness.[1] The sinful woman encountered Jesus in His incarnate humanity. Both, however, in the presence of God, became painfully aware of their sin. Both experienced the deep-felt joy of the gospel. Isaiah heard, "Your guilt is taken away, and your sin atoned for" (Isaiah 6:7). Luke did not tell us what the sinful woman heard, but undoubtedly it was some version of "Your sins, which are many, are forgiven."

Both Isaiah and the woman expressed deep heartfelt gratitude for the forgiveness of their sins. Isaiah expressed his in his grateful response to the call of God, "Whom shall I send, and who will go for us?" The sinful woman expressed hers in her daring and lavish display of worship of the One who had forgiven her.

Norval Geldenhuys, who authored an outstanding commentary on the gospel of Luke, wrote at the conclusion of his comments on the story of the sinful woman,

> All real love towards Christ must be preceded by a deep consciousness of our own sinfulness and unfitness for acceptance before the Holy God and by the assurance that for Jesus' sake our sins, however great they may be, are forgiven. Love of the Lord that is not founded upon these two foundations cannot be genuine or permanent.[2]

In more concise words I would say, "Consciousness of one's own sinfulness and assurance of forgiveness are the foundation of our love for God."

GUILT, GRACE, AND GRATITUDE

The famous Heidelberg Catechism, published in 1563, is well known for the fact that it is deliberately structured on three concepts: guilt, grace, and gratitude. I have chosen to use the word *gospel* instead of *grace*, but the idea is the same. The gospel is the message of what Christ accomplished in His life and death. Grace, as we will see in the next chapter, is the result in our lives of what He accomplished.

Guilt, gospel (or grace), and gratitude is the story line of both Isaiah's and the sinful woman's experiences. It is the story line of this book to this point, except that I have added a fourth "G": God. It is Isaiah's vision of the infinite holiness of God that awakens his painful awareness of his sin, leading him to a deep appreciation of the gospel and resulting in a joyful expression of gratitude.

In the story of the sinful woman, Jesus said, "He who is forgiven little, loves little" (Luke 7:47). This seems so descriptive of our contemporary Christian culture. Because we tend to define sin in terms of the flagrant ones in our society, we have little sense of our own personal guilt before an infinitely holy God. Consequently, we have little appreciation for the forgiveness of our sins and so little enthusiasm to earnestly pursue holiness or serve God sacrificially. There is no "guilt, grace, gratitude" sequence in most of our lives.

I realize none of us has had an Isaiah-like vision of the holiness of God, and few of us come from a notoriously sinful past as did the sinful woman. Many of us have come from Christian, or at least morally upright, homes, so it might be difficult to identify with either Isaiah or the sinful woman. The question for us then is not whether we have had an experience similar to Isaiah or the sinful woman; the question is whether we are growing more each year in our awareness of our own remaining sinfulness and, consequently, of our desperate dependence on the shed blood and righteousness of Christ.

Anglican Bishop J. C. Ryle (1816–1900), a contemporary of Charles Spurgeon, wrote, "The man whose soul is 'growing' feels his own sinfulness and unworthiness more every year.... The nearer he draws to God, and the more he sees of God's holiness and perfection, the more thoroughly is he sensible of his own countless imperfections."[3] Are we growing? Do we see more of our remaining sinfulness each succeeding year? Are we embracing the gospel daily for the forgiveness of our sins and for the crediting of Christ's righteousness to us?

Jesus said, "He who is forgiven little loves little," but the opposite, as seen in the lives of Isaiah and the sinful woman, is also true: He who is forgiven much loves much, and loving much will obey much and will serve much.

CONTROLLED BY LOVE

The apostle Paul experienced the motivation of Christ's love for him. In 2 Corinthians 5:14-15, he wrote, "The love of Christ controls us, because we have concluded this: that one has died for all, therefore all have died; and he died for all, that those who live might no longer live for themselves but for him who for their sake died and was raised." Paul said that the love of Christ [for him] controls him — that is, it exercises a strong directing or restraining influence over him. Notice the words *directing* and *restraining*.

Kenneth Wuest, who was a lecturer in Greek at Moody Bible Institute in the last century, wrote an expanded translation of the New Testament in an effort to capture more of the nuances of many Greek words. Here is how he translated 2 Corinthians 5:14: "The love which Christ has [for me] presses on me from all sides, holding me to one end and prohibiting me from considering any other, wrapping itself around me in tenderness, giving me an impelling motive."[4]

Notice that it is Paul's awareness of the love of Christ that governs and controls him. It holds him to one end, or goal, and prohibits him from considering any other. It is neither the fear of punishment nor the expectation of reward but solely being overwhelmed by the fact of Christ's love for him that so controls and governs and motivates him. And where did he see Christ's love? It was at the cross. It was his conclusion that Christ had died for us, and especially for him, for in Galatians 2:20, he wrote of "the Son of God, who loved *me* and gave himself for *me*" (emphasis added).

There is a sense in which we see elements of both Isaiah and the sinful woman in the life of Paul. Like Isaiah, he came from a rich Jewish heritage and could honestly say, "As to righteousness under the law, blameless" (Philippians 3:6). But in his own words, he was "a blasphemer, persecutor [of Christians], and insolent opponent [of Jesus]" (1 Timothy 1:13). Near the end of his life, he referred to himself as the foremost of sinners (see verse 15).

But then he had an encounter with the risen and glorified Christ on the Damascus Road. He realized to his horror that this Jesus, whom he had been blaspheming and whose followers he had been persecuting, was none other than the Son of God. But he received mercy and grace (see 1 Timothy 1:13-14). He, like Isaiah and the sinful woman, experienced the love of Christ, which pressed on him from all sides and, from that point on, governed and directed his life.

Paul experienced the same guilt, grace, and gratitude that Isaiah and the sinful woman experienced. And though few of us can identify with Isaiah, the sinful woman, or Paul in how dramatic their experiences were, we should desire the results: a response of gratitude and love toward Christ that compels and impels us to live not for ourselves but for Him who loved us and gave Himself for us.

The New Testament letters are filled with imperatives — that is, exhortations and challenges to pursue holiness, put on Christlike character, and present our bodies as living sacrifices. But these imperatives are always based on the objective truth of what Jesus did for us in His sinless life and sin-bearing death.

As a young Christian, I did not understand this. I went directly to the imperatives to learn what I was to do. And in my early years of Bible teaching, I taught from the same dutiful perspective. I would contrast the "ought tos" of Scripture with the sinful *desires* of the flesh. I taught that we should fill our minds with the "ought tos" of Scripture in order to fortify ourselves against the desires of the flesh. But the reality is that in the internal conflict between ought and desire, desire too often wins out. And even when ought wins, it is often a dutiful response rather than one of love and gratitude.

But then in the midst of what I thought would be a fruitful and rewarding ministry, the Holy Spirit began to peel back the layers of my heart to reveal something of the corruption and depravity still there. There were no "big" sins, just an ugly nest of what I call "respectable" sins.

I was driven to the gospel. Isaiah 53:6, "All we like sheep have gone astray; we have turned — every one — to his own way; and the LORD has laid on him the iniquity of us all," became my lifeline. I began to sing some of the old gospel hymns I had learned as a child. Such words as "Just as I am without one plea, but that thy blood was shed for me" and "Nothing in my hands I bring, simply to thy cross I cling" took on new meaning. I learned experientially that as a believer engaged in ministry, I still needed the gospel — every day in fact!

As I began to study the Scriptures with this new understanding, God providentially brought to my attention the writings of older generations, going all the way back to the Reformers of the sixteenth century and the Puritans of the seventeenth century, that emphasized the importance of the gospel in our transformation process. You saw just a few samples of such teaching in the previous chapter.

But let me give you a couple more, one from the eighteenth-century pen of the well-known John Newton, author of "Amazing Grace," and the other from his poet friend William Cowper.

> Our pleasure and our duty
> though opposite before,
> since we have seen his beauty
> are joined to part no more.
>
> JOHN NEWTON[5]

> To see the law by Christ fulfilled
> and hear his pardoning voice,
> changes a slave into a child
> and duty into choice.
>
> WILLIAM COWPER[6]

Yes, the Scriptures are filled with the imperatives of God's will for us. They are one of the several instruments the Holy Spirit uses to transform us. And, yes, we do have a duty to respond in obedience to those imperatives. But God wants us to *desire* to do what is our *duty* to do. He wants us to *want* to do what we *ought* to do. And it is the love of Christ as seen in the gospel — it is our response of gratitude for His grace — that gives desire to duty and changes "ought to" to "want to."

But the reality of the Christian life is that even as we come more and more to desire to do our duty, we still experience the combat between the flesh and the spirit. Though we may not understand all that Paul was saying in Romans 7:14-25, most of us can at least identify with some of Paul's words, such as "I do not understand my own actions. For I do not do what I want, but I do the very thing I hate" (verse 15) or "I find it to be a law that when I want to do right, evil lies close at hand" (verse 21).

Obviously this tension between desire and performance can cause frustration and discouragement. And the truth is, the more we grow, the more the tension between knowledge and desire and perceived progress becomes greater. This is because, as J. C. Ryle said, "the man whose soul is growing feels his own sinfulness and unworthiness more every year." How then can we keep motivated in the face of this growing tension?

The answer is through the gospel, particularly the perfect righteousness of Christ credited to us. While we are struggling daily with our tension between knowledge and desire and perceived performance, we are in fact united to Christ (in Him) in His perfect obedience. We must keep our eye on that glorious truth, and we must do it daily as we embrace the present reality of our justification: our righteous standing in Christ. Only then will we be motivated to keep pursuing holiness even in the face of the increased tension.

We have now devoted three chapters to the gospel and learned what it is, how we must daily embrace it, and how it provides the motivation for our part in our spiritual transformation. You may be wondering when we are going to get to the actual transformation process. That's coming soon. But first we need to consider the subject of grace: what it is and how we can fall into some common misunderstandings of it that can hamper the process of spiritual transformation.

FOR GROUP DISCUSSION

1. Have you ever felt a high level of gratitude for the gospel and love toward Christ? Why or why not?
2. Think about your sins for several moments. Do "big" sins come to mind? What "respectable" sins are you aware of?
3. What is the key to changing "duty" to "desire" and "ought to" to "want to"?

Understanding God's Grace

*Sin will have no dominion over you, since you are not under law
but under grace. What then? Are we to sin because we are not
under law but under grace? By no means!*

ROMANS 6:14-15

The word *grace*, in the fullness of its meaning, is one of the most precious truths in Scripture. And even in our secular American culture, John Newton's hymn "Amazing Grace" is said to be the most popular hymn of today. Yet, sad to say, the concept of grace as it is portrayed in the Bible is so frequently misunderstood. In fact, it is often perverted to mean that we may live as we please without regard to the law — that is, the moral will of God.

For example, some have been known to take Paul's words "You are not under law but under grace" to mean that we are no longer subject to the moral will of God and thus free to live as we please.

Others would not go that far but believe that God's grace means that He overlooks much of our sin or, to use a popular expression, "cuts us some slack." Others think God "grades on a curve" and, of course, since most people think they are better than others, they believe they will come out all right on the curve.

One well-meaning author who wanted to magnify God's grace even went so far as to express his concept of grace as "the idea that we are accepted and loved by God just as we are, and that God's approval does not have to be earned; it is simply there."

All of these misunderstandings of God's grace have resulted in an atmosphere of what we call "cheap grace" or "easy believism." Theologically, this attitude, or actual belief in some cases, is known as *antinomianism*, which means "against the law."

This attitude is not new. Even in the era of the apostles, Jude wrote of "ungodly people, who pervert the grace of our God into sensuality" (Jude 4). Paul anticipated a possible misunderstanding of his teaching on grace and spent the entire chapter of Romans 6 refuting it. So the attempts to pervert the grace of God into a license to sin, or to live as one pleases, is nothing new, but it is widespread today.

It is no wonder then that many pastors and Christian leaders are concerned about any emphasis on living by the gospel, or living by grace. They see it as opening the door to a more antinomian spirit that is already a curse on our culture. I understand their concern, but I believe that the solution is not to mingle works with grace but to teach the true nature of it and the biblical response to it. To say it another way, I believe that a correct understanding of God's grace and a consistent reliance on it is the only sure foundation for progress in spiritual transformation.

In 1844, Archibald Alexander, the first president of Princeton Theological Seminary, wrote a book titled *Thoughts On Religious Experience*, in which he addressed the subject of hindrances to growth in grace. (What Alexander called growth in grace is what I call spiritual transformation.) In his book, Alexander listed five hindrances to growth in grace. The last four are common hindrances that we would recognize today, but it is the first one that is worthy of our attention. He listed the first hindrance as "a defect in our belief in the freeness of divine grace." He continued, "To exercise unshaken confidence in the doctrine of gratuitous pardon is one of the most difficult things in the world; and to preach this doctrine fully without verging toward antinomianism is no easy task, and is therefore seldom done."[1] So this was a concern in the early nineteenth century just as it is today. Ministers were afraid that the preaching of grace would lead to antinomianism.

This was also true in the early seventeenth century. Episcopal bishop C. FitzSimons Allison, in his book *The Rise of Moralism,*[2] traced a trend among ministers in England at that time to combat the alarming spread of antinomianism by adding works to faith as the basis of one's standing and acceptance with God.

Back to Archibald Alexander. He continued, "But Christians cannot be but lean and feeble when deprived of their proper [nourishment]. It is by faith that the spiritual life is made to grow; and the doctrine of free grace without any mixture of human merit is the only true object of faith."[3]

Why would Alexander mention as the first hindrance to spiritual growth a defect in our belief in the freeness of divine grace? His reason can be summarized as follows: We are too prone to depending on our own performance for assurance of our acceptance with God, and we are too prone to depending on our own moral willpower for the ability to grow spiritually.

So, according to Alexander, the remedy for tendencies toward antinomianism is not to add works to grace but to continually emphasize the grace of God. But in order to do this and not open the door to cheap grace or easy believism, we need to have a correct understanding and heartfelt appreciation of the grace of God.

A CORRECT UNDERSTANDING OF GRACE

Historically, the evangelical definition of grace is "God's unmerited favor." This definition is not wrong, but I believe that it is inadequate — that it does not do justice to the concept of grace presented in the Bible.

To understand grace, we must realize we are not just undeserving of God's favor and blessing; we are all *ill deserving*. We all deserve the curse of God because none of us has abided "by all things written in the Book of the Law" (Galatians 3:10). The word *all* in this context means "absolutely all," no exceptions.

There is only one person in all of human history who has perfectly and completely obeyed the law of God: our Lord Jesus Christ, as we saw in chapter 4. In Deuteronomy 28, Moses set forth to the nation of Israel a series of blessings for obedience and curses for disobedience. Though the application was strictly for the Israelites in the Promised Land, the principle behind it is an eternal principle. God blesses obedience and curses disobedience.

But we have not completely obeyed, and even our best efforts toward obedience always fall short. None of us has ever on our best days earned the blessing of God. And, apart from Christ, we would all be under the curse. So what is the solution to our dilemma? It is found only in Christ, who, as our representative and substitute, earned the blessings for perfect obedience and suffered the curse for our disobedience.

Therefore, I believe that a biblical definition of grace is "God's blessings through Christ to people who deserve His curse." It is because of Christ and His sinless life and sin-bearing death that we do not receive the curse we deserve but instead receive the blessings from God we do not deserve.

At this point, I should clarify the relationship of "gospel" to "grace." Technically, the word *gospel* refers to a message. It is the "good news" of what God has done for us through Christ. As I indicated earlier, though, I use gospel as a shorthand expression to denote all that Christ did in His sinless life and sin-bearing death together with the fruit of His work. As seen in my definition of grace, God's grace focuses on the fruit — the blessings that come to us as a result of Christ's work. And it is important to realize that all of God's blessings to us are expressions of His grace. All of them come to us as a result of the work of Christ for us. Not a single blessing from God comes to us apart from the work of Christ on our behalf. Not even one!

In light of that understanding of God's grace, do you see how shallow and misguided such a concept of grace as God's over-looking some minor sins is? And do you see how completely the definition of grace as "the idea that we are accepted and loved by God just as we are and that God's approval does not have to be earned; it is simply there" misses the mark of describing true biblical grace?

The truth is, God's approval does have to be earned. That is what Christ did for us. The difference between God's "uncondi-tional" acceptance and the acceptance purchased for us by Christ is a massive difference. Failure to understand this leads to a critical misunderstanding of grace. A concept of grace that does not include our ill-deservedness and Christ's work for us will lead people down the wrong path of "cheap grace." But a concept that does include our ill-deservedness and Christ's work for us leads to gratitude for that grace, which leads to loving obedience.

A DAILY RELIANCE ON GRACE

It is not enough, however, to have a correct understanding of grace; we must also practice a daily reliance on it, even as believers. Let me give you two opposing views of grace for daily living as given by two different pastors.

The first pastor, in an interview, said, "I don't believe that obedience earns God's salvation of our souls, but it certainly earns God's favor in our lives."

The pastor who said those words is a good man who sincerely wants his people to live in obedience to God. He is concerned about the abuses of grace I've already described earlier, and I share his concern. Moreover, he is my Christian brother and a fellow laborer in Christ's kingdom. So, though I disagree with him, I do not quote him to criticize him.

Rather, I quote him because I believe he speaks for the vast majority of evangelical Christians. They may not have thought it out as he has, but their intuitive theology says we are saved by grace but we relate to God in this life by our works. That is what I assumed for probably the first fourteen years of my Christian life.

One of the dangers of this thinking is that it can lead people to think God owes them a reward for their obedience. Their perspective in life is, "If I do certain things, I expect God to come through for me." And when He doesn't, they think, *What's wrong? Why isn't He doing something to help me, and what more can I do?*

In the opposite direction, some people live in fear that because of their sin, God will punish them. One person wrote, "Needless to say, my walk with Jesus was one of not feeling good enough, always on the performance treadmill, and one of great fear of a God who was just waiting to pounce on me when I messed up."

This is the trap. If we think we earn God's favor by our obedience or disfavor by our disobedience, we will expect God to come through for us or, at the other extreme, will always be living in fear that "the other shoe will eventually drop."

The apostle Paul spoke to this kind of thinking when he wrote in Romans 4:4, "Now to the one who works, his wages are not counted as a gift but as his due." Paul wrote those words in the context of justification, but if we believe in the "present reality" of our justification as described in chapter 5, then Paul's words apply to our day-to-day relationship with God just as much as they do to our salvation.

The second pastor, who has been with the Lord for a number of years, wrote, "Jesus Christ bought and paid for every answer to prayer you will ever receive."[4]

That's an expression of grace. It fits well with the word *grace* as an acronym meaning God's Riches At Christ's Expense. That is similar to my definition, "God's blessings through Christ to people who deserve His curse."

The question is, do we really believe we deserve the curse of God? Do we have such a view of the holiness of God — that is, both His transcendent majesty and infinite moral purity — that we see even our "small" sins (small in our own eyes) as what R. C. Sproul calls "cosmic treason"?

I fear that in our day, even among sincere believers, we have lost sight of the exceeding sinfulness of sin. By contrast, godly men of earlier centuries saw their best deeds as falling so far short of the perfection God requires that they could be justly condemned for even their fervent prayers. And the famous nineteenth-century preacher Charles Spurgeon is quoted as saying, "All my labors are marred by sin and imperfection. As I think of every act I have ever done for God, I can only cry out, 'Oh, God, forgive the iniquity of my holy things.'"[5]

Do we see that we can never earn God's favor or blessing by our obedience considered in itself? Peter wrote that we "offer spiritual sacrifices acceptable to God through Jesus Christ" (1 Peter 2:5). Though Peter did not define "spiritual sacrifices," I think we can assume he included our worship, obedience, and service. And he says that all of that is acceptable to God only through Christ. The Puritan John Owen expressed it this way:

> Believers obey Christ as the one by whom our obedience is accepted by God. Believers know all their [works] are weak, imperfect and unable to abide in God's presence. Therefore they look to Christ as the one who bears the iniquity of their holy things, who adds incense to their prayers, gathers all the weeds from their duties, and makes them acceptable to God.[6]

We are saved by grace and receive God's favor by grace — that is, by the work of Christ on our behalf. So why should we obey if our obedience does not earn God's favor? The answer, as we have already seen, is gratitude for what God has done for us in Christ. Obedience that flows out of gratitude is the only obedience acceptable to God and is the only obedience that will bring joy to our own hearts.

THE REWARDS OF GRACE

Frequently the question is raised, "What about the New Testament teaching on the judgment seat of Christ when we must give an account of ourselves to God?" (see 2 Corinthians 5:10; Romans 14:12). There is no question that as believers we are expected to produce "good works," which I take to be both the good works of a holy life and the good works of service to God. Paul said that we have been "created in Christ Jesus for good works, which God prepared beforehand, that we should walk in them" (Ephesians 2:10).

The question, however, is do these good works earn any merit with God? The answer, if we believe that even our best deeds are defiled and imperfect, is that all merit is ascribed to Christ alone. Consequently, all rewards to us from God are due strictly to His grace alone.

Lefèvre d'Étaples (pronounced Luferah Daytapplah), a Frenchman who lived 1455–1536 and was a forerunner of the Protestant Reformation, wrote,

> It is sheer profanity to speak of the merit of works, especially in the presence of God. For plainly merit does not ask a favor but demands what is due.... If merit is to be attributed to anyone, it is properly and completely attributed to Christ, who has merited everything for us, while we were confessing that before God we deserve nothing, look to him for grace.[7]

Similarly Martin Bucer (1491–1551), a German contemporary of John Calvin, wrote,

That the Lord rewards his people for their good works is not on the grounds of their righteousness, but purely from his free grace, and for the sake of his dear Son, in whom he chose us for eternal life before the foundation of the world, and created us for good works, which through him he affects in us (John 15:5) and rewards so generously. Consequently, when God rewards our good works he is rewarding his works and gifts in us, rather than our own works.[8]

Keep in mind that these statements about the relationship of grace and rewards were written in the early sixteenth century. But even as far back as Isaiah, written seven hundred years before Christ, the prophet wrote, "O LORD...you have indeed done for us all our works" (Isaiah 26:12). And when Paul and Barnabas returned from their missionary journey, "they declared [to the church at Antioch] all that God had done with them, and how he had opened a door of faith to the Gentiles" (Acts 14:27). And later Paul would write, "To me, though I am the very least of all the saints, this grace [this ill-deserved privilege] was given, to preach to the Gentiles the unsearchable riches of Christ" (Ephesians 3:8). So let us stop thinking about our rewards and focus entirely on the grace of God, given to us through Christ Jesus. And then, out of gratitude, let us obey Him and serve Him with all of our hearts.

GRACE AND TRANSFORMATION

If we think of grace as God's blessings (note the plural) through Christ, then we realize that His grace is dynamic. It is not just a benevolent attitude but God acting for our good. And in a broad sense, all the various expressions of grace in the Bible can be summarized under two major headings: privileges and power. Sometimes Paul used both privilege and power in the same sentence or two so that he effectively merged them together. Consider, for example, 1 Corinthians 15:9-10:

> I am the least of the apostles, unworthy to be called an apostle, because I persecuted the church of God. But by the grace of God I am what I am, and his grace toward me was not in vain. On the contrary, I worked harder than any of them, though it was not I, but the grace of God that is with me.

First he spoke of God's grace as the undeserved privilege of being an apostle, and at the same time he spoke of His grace working so effectively in him, an obvious reference to His power. That God sometimes equates His grace with His power is brought out clearly in 2 Corinthians 12:9, which states that God said to Paul, "My grace is sufficient for you, for my power is made perfect in weakness." But God's power always comes to us through Christ and by the Holy Spirit. It is Christ who has merited for us the power of God, and it is by the ministry of the Holy Spirit in us that His power is applied to us and becomes a working force in our lives. That is why Paul prayed to the Father "that according to the riches of his glory he may grant you to be strengthened with power through his Spirit in your inner being" (Ephesians 3:16).

Paul wrote to Timothy, "You then, my child, be strengthened by the grace that is in Christ Jesus" (2 Timothy 2:1). The verb *be strengthened* is what is called (in grammar) a present passive. *Present* means a continuous, ongoing action. *Passive* means something is done to the subject. We might render Paul's words this way: "Be continually strengthened by a source of strength from outside of you." And what is this source? It is "the grace that is in Christ Jesus." It is the power of God coming to us through Christ and applied to us by the Holy Spirit.

It is important that we see God's power as an expression of His grace, for we have now reached a transition point in our study of gospel-based transformation. Up to now, we have focused on the gospel as the foundation and motivation for our pursuit of spiritual transformation. Beginning in the next chapter, we will focus on the process, and critical to that process is the work of the Holy Spirit to work in us and to enable us to work. That is why the content of the next chapter focuses on the transforming work of the Holy Spirit. And, remember, this transforming work is an expression of God's grace just as much as is our salvation.

FOR GROUP DISCUSSION

1. What forms of "cheap grace" or "easy believism" have you encountered or embraced in the past?
2. What is it preachers fear most when they preach a message of grace? How would you answer that fear?
3. Good works, holy living, and service are all part of the Christian life, but do they earn us merit with God? Why or why not?

CHAPTER EIGHT

The Transforming Work of the Holy Spirit

We all, with unveiled face, beholding the glory of the Lord, are being transformed into the same image from one degree of glory to another. For this comes from the LORD who is the Spirit.

2 CORINTHIANS 3:18

The transformation process the Bible describes is much more than a change of conduct or improved human morality; it is actually a work of the Holy Spirit in the very core of our being. In the only two instances in Scripture where the word *transformed* is used, it occurs both times in the passive voice. We are *being* transformed (see 2 Corinthians 3:18), and we are to *be* transformed (see Romans 12:2). In both instances, we are the object, not the agent, of the transformation process; the agent is the Holy Spirit.

We do have an active role to play in this process. All the moral exhortations and commands in the New Testament assume our responsibility to respond to them. We will look more at our responsibility in the next two chapters, but for now we want to focus on the role and work of the Holy Spirit. We need to do this for two reasons. First, just as we are naturally inclined to depend on our own performance for our day-to-day relationship with God, so we are also inclined to depend on our own willpower and our "try harder" way of thinking to effect change in our character.

So just as we must look outside of ourselves to Christ rather than our own performance for the assurance of our acceptance by a holy God, so we must look outside of ourselves to the Holy Spirit to work in us and enable us to work. In chapter 1, I related how, in my early stages of pursuing holiness, I simply assumed I would read in the Bible what God wanted me to do and do it. I knew nothing of my actual dependence on the Holy Spirit to enable me. I suspect that a majority of Christians intuitively believe as I did because they have not been taught differently.

The second reason we need to consider the role of the Holy Spirit in our transformation is that some of the extreme, erroneous teaching about Him has made many of us very cautious of His work in our lives. But we neglect the work of the Holy Spirit to our detriment. After all, He is the resident member of the Trinity in us. As incredible as it may seem, our bodies are the temple of the Holy Spirit (see 1 Corinthians 6:19). Think of that! The Holy Spirit, one of the three persons of the Trinity, actually dwells within you. And Christ Himself dwells within you through the Holy Spirit (see Ephesians 3:16-17).

In Christ, "the whole fullness of deity dwells bodily" (Colossians 2:9). All that God has for us and all that He has purposed for us is in Christ. He is the vine; we are the branches (see John 15:5). But it is the role of the Holy Spirit to apply the life and power of Christ to us. As someone has so aptly said, "the Spirit applies what Christ bestows." We cannot experience one drop of the life and power of Christ apart from the work of the Spirit in our lives.

In the matter of our transformation, the writers of Scripture sometimes spoke of God's working in us, at other times of Christ's working in us, or even make an indefinite reference to "Him" as in "I can do all things through him who strengthens me" (Philippians 4:13). But in all cases, it is the role of the Holy Spirit to apply and work out in our lives that which comes to us from God through Christ. So though the persons of Christ and the Holy Spirit are distinct, in our transformation experience they are indistinguishable. So we may speak of the power of Christ and the power of the Holy Spirit as interchangeable expressions. But because it is the role of the Spirit to apply to us what the Father has purposed and what Christ has obtained for us, we will focus in this chapter on the transforming work of the Holy Spirit.

THE AUTHOR OF SCRIPTURE

As we begin our study of the work of the Spirit, we should see Him first as the author of Scripture. We speak of the Bible as the Word of God, and so it is, for as Paul wrote, "All Scripture is breathed out by God" (2 Timothy 3:16). But God did this through the Holy Spirit. As Peter wrote, "Men spoke from God as they were carried along by the Holy Spirit" (2 Peter 1:21). That means that the Holy Spirit infallibly guided the minds of the human writers of Scripture so they wrote exactly what He wanted them to write. That is why we find such expressions as "The Holy Spirit spoke beforehand by the mouth of David" (Acts 1:16; see also 4:25; 28:25-27; Hebrews 3:7-11; 10:15-17).

So just as God created the universe through the eternal Son of God (see John 1:3; Colossians 1:16; Hebrews 1:2), so He gave us His Word through the eternal Spirit. In a subsequent chapter, we will see that Scripture is the primary instrument of the Holy Spirit as He works to transform us. That is why we stress the importance of the Scriptures in our spiritual growth (see chapter 11). But we must keep in mind that it is the Holy Spirit who gave us the Scriptures, it is the Holy Spirit who enables us to understand the Scriptures, and it is the Holy Spirit who directs us and enables us to apply the Scriptures to our daily lives.

THE AGENT OF THE NEW BIRTH

As descendents of Adam and because of his sin in the Garden of Eden, we are "born dead." As Paul said in Ephesians 2:1-2, "You were dead in the trespasses and sins in which you once walked." But a few sentences later, he wrote, "God, being rich in mercy, because of the great love with which he loved us, even when we were dead in our trespasses, made us alive together with Christ" (verses 4-5). When we were dead, God made us alive. How did He do this? Jesus' answer in John 3:5-8 is that we are born again by the Spirit. And Paul wrote that God saved us "by the washing of regeneration and renewal of the Holy Spirit" (Titus 3:5). The word *regeneration* means "born again," so our new birth is again ascribed to the Holy Spirit.

Peter said that we are "born again . . . through the living and abiding word of God" (1 Peter 1:23). So we are born again by the Spirit and by the Word of God. But remember, the Spirit is the ultimate author of the Word, and so it is the instrument He uses to bring about the new birth in our lives. But apart from the renewing work of the Spirit, the Word remains lifeless.

I grew up hearing the message of the gospel regularly. I knew I needed to ask Christ to be my Savior, but because of a disappointing circumstance when I was about thirteen, I held back. In one sense, I wanted to be a Christian, but there was this obstacle from the past I couldn't get over. I lived this way for five years. Finally one night at the age of eighteen, I prayed, "God, whatever it takes, I want Jesus to be my Savior." Immediately the Spirit bore witness with my spirit that I was a child of God (see Romans 8:15). The Word of God by itself was not enough. I knew the gospel, but because of that issue at age thirteen, I held back. What happened at age eighteen? The Spirit of God so worked in me that I was willing to deal with that obstacle. I was born again by the Spirit of God.

THE WITNESS TO OUR ADOPTION

In Ephesians 1:4-6, Paul wrote, "In love [God] predestined us for adoption through Jesus Christ, according to the purpose of his will, to the praise of his glorious grace." What did Paul mean by *adoption* in this passage? He meant that God not only has justified us, He has also brought us into His family as His own sons and daughters. *Justification* describes our *legal* relationship with God; *adoption* describes our *family* relationship with Him. Through our union with Christ, God sees us as righteous — as righteous as His Son. And also through our union with Christ, God sees us as His adopted children. This means, among other things, that God loves us with the same love He has for His Son because we are united to Him.

It is important that we realize that God relates to us no longer as a sovereign judge but now as our heavenly Father. A judge punishes to satisfy justice, but Jesus has already satisfied God's justice on our behalf. A father disciplines through love to grow his children's character, and this is the way God relates to us as His adopted children.

A necessary part of the Holy Spirit's transformation work in us is to enlighten our minds to progressively see and become more sensitive to the sin still remaining in us, either sinful attitudes and actions we need to put off or fruit of the Spirit traits we need to grow in. Because of this, we need the assurance that despite our continual sinfulness, we still stand righteous before God every day. But we also need the assurance that God is for us, and this is where the Spirit's witness to our adoption is so important.

In Romans 8:15, Paul wrote, "You did not receive the spirit of slavery to fall back into fear, but you have received the Spirit of adoption as sons, by whom we cry, 'Abba! Father!'" Here Paul calls the Spirit "the Spirit of adoption." It is the Holy Spirit that witnesses to our spirit that we are God's children. It is the Holy Spirit by whom we cry, "Abba! Father!" Abba was the Aramaic address of small children to their fathers; thus, it was a term of intimate relationship and confidence. The modern English equivalent to Abba is *daddy*. If that seems too chummy and maybe irreverent to you, I suggest you address God as "dear Father." That will maintain the sense of reverence while at the same time give you more of a sense of loving intimacy than simply "Father."

Far too many Christians view God as a stern, aloof Father ready to pounce on them when they sin. If this is your view of God, I encourage you to pray that the Holy Spirit will witness to you of the joy and comfort that should be yours as God's adopted child. And the deliberate practice of addressing God as "dear Father" will help you. As you grow in understanding your adoption, you will be motivated by God's love to deal with your sin.

THE AGENT OF SANCTIFICATION

The word *sanctification* is not common in our Christian vocabulary today, especially among younger believers. And even when it is used, it is generally used as another word for transformation or spiritual growth. In fact, that is the most common way it is used. But the Bible relates sanctification to our salvation. Notice how it is used in the following two Scriptures:

> We ought always to give thanks to God for you, brothers beloved by the Lord, because God chose you as the firstfruits to be saved, through sanctification by the Spirit and belief in the truth. To this he called you through our gospel, so that you may obtain the glory of our Lord Jesus Christ. (2 Thessalonians 2:13-14)

> Peter, an apostle of Jesus Christ, To those who are elect exiles of the dispersion in Pontus, Galatia, Cappadocia,

Asia, and Bithynia, according to the foreknowledge of God the Father, in the sanctification of the Spirit, for obedience to Jesus Christ and for sprinkling with his blood: May grace and peace be multiplied to you. (1 Peter 1:1-2)

Note in both texts the reference to "sanctification by the Spirit" (2 Thessalonians) or "the sanctification of the Spirit" (1 Peter). The New International Version helpfully renders both texts "the sanctifying work of the Spirit." But notice that this sanctifying work of the Spirit is in conjunction with our salvation. Why is this true?

The basic meaning of the verb *to sanctify* is to set apart — in this case, to set apart unto God for His use. Paul wrote that Jesus "gave himself for us to redeem us from all lawlessness and to purify for himself a people for *his own possession*" (Titus 2:14, emphasis added). Peter used identical words in 1 Peter 2:9: "You are a chosen race, a royal priesthood, a holy nation, a people for *his own possession*" (emphasis added). This sanctifying work is the work of the Holy Spirit by which He delivers us from the domain of darkness (see Colossians 1:13) and sets us apart to be Christ's own possession. The Spirit not only gives us a new spiritual life (the new birth) but also sets us apart to be Christ's possession. Obviously, these acts of the Holy Spirit occur simultaneously with our salvation. Remember, God's purpose in our salvation is that we might be conformed to the image of His Son. Those whom God justifies, the Holy Spirit sanctifies.

This aspect of sanctification is often called definitive sanctification because it is an objective point-in-time event accomplished solely by the Holy Spirit. Those who are thus sanctified are called "saints" (see, for example, 1 Corinthians 1:2; 2 Corinthians 1:1; Philippians 1:1). The word *saints* literally means "set apart ones," and in this biblical meaning of the word, all believers are saints.

But the status of saint is not so much a position of honor but of responsibility. Because we have been set apart by the Holy Spirit to be Christ's own possession, we are to live as unto Him. As Paul wrote to the Corinthians, "You are not your own, for you were bought with a price" (1 Corinthians 6:19-20). This thought naturally leads us to the subject of transformation, or "progressive sanctification," as some prefer to call it. That is, because we are set apart to be Christ's own possession, we are to seek to live more and more in our daily experience lives that reflect this fact. We call this the pursuit of holiness, or the pursuit of Christlikeness. So at this point, we begin to transition to discussion of our responsibility in our transformation. But even as we do, we cannot leave behind the Holy Spirit because we are still dependent on Him. Remember, as we saw earlier, in both instances where the word *transformed* is used, it is in the passive voice.

THE AGENT OF TRANSFORMATION

As the agent of our transformation, the Holy Spirit both works in us and enables us to work. As the writer of Hebrews expressed it, "[May God] equip you with everything good that you may do his will, working in us that which is pleasing in his sight, through Jesus Christ, to whom be glory forever and ever. Amen" (13:20-21).

The writer prayed that God would do two things: equip us to do his will and work in us that which is pleasing in His sight. So God through the Holy Spirit equips us to do what we must do, and He also works directly in us that which is pleasing to Him. I call these two aspects of His work His synergistic work and His monergistic work. Synergism refers to two persons working together; monergism is one person working alone.

When we pray that God will change us in some area of our lives, we are asking for His monergistic work. For example, the writer of Psalm 119 prayed, "Incline my heart to your testimonies, and not to selfish gain! Turn my eyes from looking at worthless things" (verses 36-37). The psalmist is asking God to do for him and to him what he cannot do for himself. He is asking that God through His Spirit will work monergistically in him. We know that to some degree, we can change our conduct but not our hearts, that is, the deep inner core of our being. Only the Holy Spirit can do this, and He does it monergistically.

How does the Holy Spirit bring about these kinds of changes? He works monergistically in at least three ways:

He Brings Conviction

The first way the Holy Spirit works directly in us is by bringing conviction of, or an awareness of, specific sin in our lives. It is obvious that we cannot begin to deal with a specific issue of sin until we first admit that we have it. Only the Holy Spirit can create such awareness, and He has different ways of doing that. He may impress on our minds a particular passage of Scripture as we are reading our Bibles or listening to a message. He causes us to connect the Scripture to a specific issue in our lives in such a way that we see the application and readily acknowledge the existence of the sin in our character.

He awakens and sensitizes our conscience. The conscience is our internal moral compass, and as it is enlightened through the Scriptures, it will continually convict us of sinful attitudes and actions.

He may bring to our remembrance a series of seemingly insignificant sins to cause us to see that those individual sins are simply an expression of a pattern in our lives. Again, He does this in such a way that we readily acknowledge that defect in our character. He may even use adversity to get our attention and cause us to acknowledge we have a sin problem. Sometimes He sends a friend or relative, especially a spouse, to point out a sin issue in our lives. This is probably the most painful way to us. We don't like to be corrected. So unless the Spirit softens our hearts and makes us receptive, we will often resent, or at least dismiss, the correction.

Above all, He gradually brings us to the realization that we are indeed still sinners, saved sinners, to be sure, but still *practicing* sinners every day in thought, word, deed, and motive. He brings us to the point where we say with the apostle Paul, "Christ Jesus came into the world to save sinners, of whom I am the foremost" (1 Timothy 1:15). This is where change begins.

He Creates Desire

Having brought us to the point of seeing our need for change, the Holy Spirit works in us to create the desire to change. Actually, we may desire to change for the wrong reason, either because we don't like to feel guilty or because we don't like to feel defeated by some persistent sin pattern. But the Holy Spirit works in us to create a God-centered desire to change. He does this through a combination of showing us our sin and at the same time enabling us to experience the forgiveness of our sins and the gift of Christ's righteousness credited to us. Of course, one of the instruments He uses is the gospel to motivate us, but even here we are dependent on Him. We may "preach the gospel to ourselves every day," but unless the Holy Spirit grips our hearts with the reality of that good news, we will not be motivated by it. So we should pray to Him to do this. I pray almost every day that Christ will so control me by His love that I will want to change to please Him. (You might want to reread the section "Controlled by Love" in chapter 6.)

He Creates Change

After making us aware of our need and creating a desire to change, the Holy Spirit works on our hearts to bring about change. In this aspect of His work, He works directly, mysteriously (in the sense that we cannot discern how He works), and without our awareness or conscious involvement. I cannot explain this; I can only testify to the reality of it in my life. I believe this is what the writer of Hebrews was getting at when he wrote, "[May he work] in us that which is pleasing in his sight" (13:21).

We are commanded to love one another, yet there are times when, because of the personality or actions of another person, we find it impossible to love that person. But as we pray that God will change us, we see a new, loving attitude created in our hearts. This is the monergistic work of the Spirit. I have experienced this in my life. A person I found difficult to love became a good friend. Did he change? No. The Holy Spirit changed me.

In my book *Respectable Sins*, I acknowledged that I am prone to anxiety in connection with airline travel. I'm not talking about a fear of flying; I'm referring to anxiety over delayed flights that will cause me to miss a connecting flight or else cause me to arrive too late for a meeting where I am to speak. And then there are times when my checked bag does not arrive on the same flight with me. Both of these situations happened to me the week I was writing these words, so I struggled with anxiety, first over whether I would make a connecting flight to my destination. Then when my bag did not arrive with me, I again struggled with anxiety. Would my bag arrive by the time I needed it?

I knew very well that we are not to be anxious. I know that God is sovereign over every circumstance of my life and that He loves me with an infinite love, yet I cannot change my feelings of anxiety. But as I prayed, the Holy Spirit enabled me to trust God, at least to a measure. This is still a growth area in my life, but I can see over time that the Holy Spirit is changing me.

I cite these instances of loving a person difficult to love and anxiety over my travel circumstances to point out that there are instances when we cannot change ourselves. We can to a degree change our conduct; we can seek to be nice to the person difficult to love, but we cannot change our heart attitude. I can quote Scripture to myself regarding the sovereignty and love of God, but I cannot still my anxious heart. Only the Holy Spirit can do both of these: create love in me toward the unlovely person and calm my anxious emotions.

I have perhaps belabored these incidents from my own life, but it is because I want us to see that the direct work of the Holy Spirit, working alone without our involvement, is a crucial part of our spiritual transformation. It is important for us to realize this, thank Him for His work, and regularly pray for it. In fact, Paul's prayers in Ephesians 3:14-19 and Colossians 1:9-12 assume the Spirit's direct work in us. Too often we pay so much attention to what we need to do (the subject of the next chapter) that we totally neglect the extent to which we are entirely dependent on the Spirit to do what we cannot do.

THE SPIRIT'S WORK OF ENABLEMENT

As we read the New Testament and see the many moral exhortations and commands throughout the whole of it, we must surely be convinced that there is work for us to do. But we have a problem: We have no power to do the work. So now we must turn our attention to His work of enabling us to work — that is, His synergistic work.

Jesus said in John 15:5, "Apart from me you can do nothing." Nothing? That's right. Nothing. Picture a large electric motor designed to drive a large machine, such as a lathe. You turn on the switch and nothing happens. Why? The motor has not been connected to the source of power: the 220-volt electric current in the machine shop. That large motor has absolutely no power within itself. To work, it must be connected to an external power source (the 220-volt current). If we personify the electric current and the motor, we can use Jesus' exact words in the current saying to the motor, "Apart from me you can do nothing."

This is the way we are. God has given us a new heart (see Ezekiel 36:26), and that new heart can be likened to the electric motor. It has no power of itself. The power resides in the Holy Spirit, who lives in each believer (see Ezekiel 36:27;

1 Corinthians 6:19). How do we then connect to the power of the Spirit? We do it by faith — by renouncing any confidence in our own willpower and relying entirely on the Holy Spirit to empower us.

ABIDING = RELIANCE

In John 15:4-5, Jesus made it clear that the divine source of life and power comes through abiding in Him. But how does one abide?

Most often we think of activities such as studying our Bible and praying as abiding in Christ. These are important spiritual activities that I will address in chapter 10. But these activities do not constitute abiding in Christ; rather, they belong in a subject we call communion with Christ. What then does it mean to abide in Christ? It is *reliance* on Him for His life and His power. By faith we renounce any confidence in our own wisdom, willpower, and moral strength and rely completely on Him to supply the spiritual wisdom and power we need. This does not mean we sit back and just "turn it all over to Him" to live His life through us; rather, we rely on Him to enable us (we'll examine this more in the next chapter). So we can say that our salvation is by faith and our transformation is also by faith. But this does not mean that the object of our faith is the same in both cases.

In salvation, the object of our faith is Christ and His finished work *for* us. When He uttered those memorable words "It is finished" (John 19:30), it was a cry of triumph that the salvation which He had earned *for* us in His sinless life and sin-bearing death had been completely accomplished. There was nothing more for Him to do. And in trusting Him for our salvation, there is nothing for us to do except receive Him by faith.

By contrast, the object of our faith in spiritual transformation is Christ and His ongoing work *in* us through the Holy Spirit. In our transformation, then, there is something for us to do. In salvation, we are passive except to believe. In transformation, we are active as we seek to pursue holiness in relying on the Holy Spirit to apply the power of Christ to our hearts and enable us to do His will.

You will no doubt have noticed that I have devoted more emphasis in this chapter to the direct monergistic ministry of the Spirit in us as opposed to His synergistic work of enabling us to work. There are two reasons for this. First, we are going to devote the entire next chapter to His work of enabling us. Second, I believe we have tended to pay too little attention to His direct, monergistic ministry. We tend to think so much of what we need to do that we seldom think of our dependence on the Spirit to even enable us, let alone work monergistically and directly in our hearts to change us.

Dependence on the Holy Spirit has been a growing process for me. In chapter 1, I recounted how I had embraced for a time a totally passive approach to spiritual growth, with its slogan "Just let Jesus live His life through you." As God rescued me from this thinking, I began to understand the biblical principle of dependent responsibility, meaning I am responsible for my pursuit of holiness but am dependent on the Holy Spirit for His enabling power. Because of my previous bad experience with the totally passive approach, my concept of dependent responsibility put the emphasis on my responsibility. Written out, it would look like this: "dependent RESPONSIBILITY."

Over time I came to realize more deeply how utterly dependent on the Holy Spirit I am for every bit of my spiritual growth. Gradually, my concept of the relationship of dependence and responsibility came to look like this: "DEPENDENT RESPONSIBILITY." But even at this stage, I was not so aware of the necessity of the Holy Spirit's working directly in me to change me in ways I cannot.

You might ask, "How does He work in us, either monergistically or synergistically, to enable us to work?" The answer is, we do not know, as the Bible never addresses that question. Paul wrote, "The Spirit himself bears witness with our spirit that we are children of God" (Romans 8:16), but he never tells us how the Holy Spirit interacts with our human spirit to create this assurance. He simply says He does this. And as we will see in the next chapter, He does work in us to enable us to work, but the Scripture never tells us how. How He works in us remains a mystery, but the fact that He does work is not a mystery. It is a fact, as we will see in the next chapter, "Dependent Responsibility."

FOR GROUP DISCUSSION

1. What role does the Holy Spirit play in our transformation? How is this role distinct from that of the Father and the Son?
2. What is the monergistic work of the Holy Spirit? How is it different from His synergistic work?
3. The object of our faith in spiritual transformation is Christ and His ongoing work *in* us through the Holy Spirit. How is this different from the object of our faith for salvation?

CHAPTER NINE

Dependent Responsibility

My beloved, as you have always obeyed, so now, not only as in my presence but much more in my absence, work out your own salvation with fear and trembling, for it is God who works in you, both to will and to work for his good pleasure.

PHILIPPIANS 2:12-13

The Scripture that expresses most plainly the principle of dependent responsibility is Philippians 2:12-13, above. Verse 12 says we are to work out our salvation; that is, we are to work out in our daily lives the new life that has been implanted within us at the time of our salvation. This is our responsibility. But verse 13 tells us that we can do this because God is at work in us, both to will and to work. This verse not only implies our dependence but actually assures us that we can work because God is at work in us.

We find this principle in the Old Testament in Psalm 127:1: "Unless the LORD builds the house, those who build it labor in vain. Unless the LORD watches over the city, the watchman stays awake in vain." Two activities are mentioned: building and watching. In a general sense, these two activities describe our role in transformation. We should always be proactively "building"

Christian character in our lives. At the same time, we should be "watching" over our lives to guard against temptation.

As we examine this verse, note first of all what the psalmist did not say. He did not speak of the Lord helping the builder or the watchman. Rather, he spoke of God actually building the house and watching over the city. At the same time, the builder is still laboring and the watchman is still watching.

There is no question that they must fulfill their respective responsibilities. They cannot "just turn it over to the Lord" and let Him build or watch. No, they must do their work. But all of their building and watching activities are in vain unless the Lord builds and watches. So what is the psalmist teaching us? He is teaching us that we are both fully responsible and fully dependent.

The apostle Paul expressed this principle of dependent responsibility in both his life and his ministry. Concerning his life, he said, "I can do all things through him who strengthens me" (Philippians 4:13). In context, "all things" refers to his personal life. But in Colossians 1:29, he spoke of his ministry. There he said, "For this [that is, his ministry] I toil, struggling with all his energy that he powerfully works within me." The word *toil* implies working to the point of exhaustion. The word *struggling* is from the Greek word from which we get our word *agonize*. Toil refers to Paul's activities of proclaiming, warning, and teaching (see verse 28). His struggling apparently refers to his prayer life because he used the same word when he wrote of Epaphras struggling in prayer (see Colossians 4:12). Both *toil* and *struggling* are strong, vigorous words indicating the intensity with which Paul engaged in his ministry as he both preached and prayed. But he did it in full dependence on Christ's energy, which worked so powerfully within him.

Paul recognized he was responsible, so he labored to the point of physical exhaustion. But he also recognized he was fully depen-dent on the power of Christ to make his work effective, so he struggled (agonized) in prayer that Christ would work in him and through him.

The age of the English Puritans in the seventeenth century was undoubtedly the most influential era of English evangelicalism. Their books and sermons, even with their difficult-to-read prose, are still being reprinted, read, and profited from today in all the English-speaking nations. The Puritans understood the concept of dependent responsibility. They used to say (and this is not an exact quote but captures their attitude), "Work as if it all depends on you, yet pray as if it all depends on God." They labored diligently to become more like Christ, but they also prayed diligently because they knew they were dependent on the Holy Spirit to make their labor effective. This is the way we apply the principle of dependent responsibility.

PROVERBS

Proverbs 2:1-5 is another Scripture passage that so aptly describes what I mean by the expression *dependent responsibility*. But the reason I have included it in this chapter is because it also introduces another character trait necessary for our transformation: a teachable spirit. Here is the entire passage for your convenience:

> My son, if you receive my words
>   and treasure up my commandments with you,
> making your ear attentive to wisdom
>   and inclining your heart to understanding;
> yes, if you call out for insight
>   and raise your voice for understanding,
> if you seek it like silver
>   and search for it as for hidden treasures,
> then you will understand the fear of the LORD
>   and find the knowledge of God.

In this passage, Solomon gave three necessary characteristics of the person who would understand the fear of God. Because I do not want to pursue the subject of the fear of God at this time, let me say that a simple definition of that term is "a profound reverence for God that results in a life that is seeking to please God." So the passage really is relevant to our subject of spiritual transformation, of seeking to please God through the pursuit of holiness.

The first characteristic Solomon said is necessary is a *teachable spirit* (see verse 1). The person with this attitude receives his Father's words and treasures up His commandments in his heart. He is not only open to instruction, he treasures it.

TEACHABLE SPIRIT

A teachable spirit begins with a spirit of humility that recognizes that we know so little of God's Word and apply even less of what we do know. It is a spirit that recognizes that we have so much sin remaining in us, especially in those areas I call "respectable sins." It is a spirit that recognizes how much we need to grow in those character traits Paul called the fruit of the Spirit: love, joy, peace, forbearance, kindness, goodness, faithfulness, gentleness, and self-control (see Galatians 5:22-23).

In short, a teachable spirit is descriptive of a person who knows he or she needs to change and grow and is eager to do so. This person approaches the Bible not simply to acquire knowledge but to apply that knowledge to his life. In our modern English translation of the Bible, the word *knowledge* is often used for two different Greek words, *ginosko* and *epiginosko*. The first word is used for acquiring bare knowledge or truth. The second word obviously builds on the first but suggests a fuller perception and application of the knowledge.

We see the difference in the two words in Paul's use of them in 1 Corinthians 8:1 and Colossians 1:9. In the former passage, Paul used the Greek word *ginosko*, which our Bible translates as "knowledge." The Corinthians "knew" that "'an idol has no real existence,' and that 'there is no God but one'" (1 Corinthians 8:4). Paul did not dispute the correctness of their knowledge. Their problem was not a lack of knowledge; it was in the misapplication of that knowledge in the area of Christian liberty and Christian love.

By contrast, in Colossians 1:9, where Paul said he prayed "that you might be filled with the *knowledge* of [God's] will in all spiritual wisdom and understanding" (emphasis added), he used the word *epiginosko*. He wants them to participate in this knowledge by applying it to their lives.

Paul also used *epiginosko* in Titus 1:1, where he spoke of "[our] knowledge of the truth, which accords with godliness," or, as other translations render it, "knowledge of the truth, which leads to godliness." Which direction is our knowledge of Scripture taking us? Is it taking us in the direction of pride, in which we know so much yet fail to apply it to our lives or even misapply it? Or is our knowledge of Scripture taking us in the direction of not only knowing but doing His will in a way that leads to growth in godliness?

These questions are pertinent to the spirit of teachability and consequently to our transformation. We are not truly teachable unless our desire to learn more of the Bible is motivated by a sincere desire to grow in Christlikeness, not by a satisfaction that we know so much of Bible facts and doctrine. We can easily fool ourselves with our intellectual knowledge (our *ginosko*) while failing to enter into a genuine experience and application of that knowledge (*epigonosko*).

DILIGENT ATTITUDE

A teachable spirit, however, is not enough. It must be accompanied by an attitude of diligence — an attitude that seeks instruction from the Scriptures as one seeking for valuable treasure. It is an attitude that stimulates us to action and leads us to grow in our Christian lives. The apostle Peter, after assuring us of the power and promises available to us (see 2 Peter 1:2-4), urged and exhorted us to "make every effort" (or, as the NASB says, "[apply] all diligence") to supplement our faith with various Christian character traits (see 2 Peter 1:5-7). Think of the picture of diligence and hard work implied in the words of Proverbs 2:4: "Seek [wisdom] like silver and search for it as for hidden treasures."

A related word in the Greek language is translated in 2 Timothy 2:15 as "Do your best." In Hebrews 4:11, it is translated as "Strive to enter [God's] rest." "Do your best" and "strive" — these are strong, vigorous words. Do they describe your pursuit of holiness, or have you reached a certain level of acceptable Christian conduct and plateaued in your spiritual growth? Are you more loving, more patient, more compassionate, more generous with your money, more ready to forgive wrongs against you than you were a year ago?

What is it then that will stimulate us and motivate us to pursue holiness with all the vigor implied in such phrases as "make every effort," "be diligent," "do your best," "strive," "seek as for silver," or "search as for hidden treasures"? To this we go back to chapter 6, "The Motivation of the Gospel." A pursuit of holiness that is not based on gospel motivation will soon become a duty rather than a delight. And it may well lead to religious pride because we gauge our holiness by respectable religious conduct, or it may lead to discouragement and even despair because we are not living up to our own expectations, let alone what we assume to be God's expectations.

PAUL'S EXAMPLE

Because this is such a major issue, let's go back to the subject of gospel motivation as we see it in the life of the apostle Paul.

In Philippians 3:4-9, Paul described how he changed dramatically from the life of a zealous but self-righteous Pharisee to a life of depending entirely on the righteousness of Christ (see verse 9). What effect did this have on Paul? Did it cause him to say, "Since I'm righteous in Christ it doesn't matter how I live"? Absolutely not! Here are his words as recorded in Philippians 3:12-14:

> Not that I have already obtained this or am already perfect, but I press on to make it my own, because Christ Jesus has made me his own. Brothers, I do not consider that I have made it my own. But one thing I do: forgetting what lies behind and straining forward to what lies ahead, I press on toward the goal for the prize of the upward call of God in Christ Jesus.

Note the strong and intense verbs Paul used to describe his life as one who was righteous in Christ Jesus. The phrase *press on* in verses 12 and 14 is elsewhere translated as *pursue* (see 1 Timothy 6:11 and 2 Timothy 2:22). It is the same Greek word that in a different context means *persecute*. In fact, Paul used the same word in Philippians 3:6, where referring to his previous life as a Pharisee he said, "As to zeal, a persecutor of the church."

Paul had this same zeal he had as a Pharisee, but now it was directed toward becoming all God intended him to be in Christ Jesus. In verse 13, Paul used a different picture — that of a runner straining with all his energy to cross the finish line first. As you visualize such a race from the vantage point of the finish line, you can see the look of intensity and sometimes agony on the faces of the runners. This was Paul in his own personal pursuit of holiness. Remember that Paul wrote these words from a position of house arrest in Rome. In the letter to Philemon, he referred to himself as an old man (see Philemon 9), yet in Philippians 3, he displayed the same zeal and intensity as a young man running a race in the Grecian games of that day.

What kept this zeal burning in Paul's heart? It was the daily appropriation of the gospel. When in verse 9 he spoke of having a righteousness of his own that comes not from [obedience to] the law but rather through faith in Christ, he was not speaking of a past event of being saved but of a daily reality of appropriating by faith the infinitely perfect righteousness of Christ. And daily realizing that he was righteous in Christ spurred him on to seek to be in his daily experience what he was in his standing in Christ. A daily appropriation of the gospel, in which we see that our sins are forgiven and that we stand before God clothed in the spotless righteousness of Christ, is the key to the diligent pursuit of holiness.

DEPENDENT ATTITUDE

But as we saw back in Proverbs 2, diligence assumes dependence: "Yes, if you call out for insight and raise your voice for understanding" (verse 3). Calling out and raising one's voice are pictorial expressions of prayer, and prayer should be a concrete expression of our dependence (though often our prayers are no more than a wish list presented to God). When we are on our knees (at least in our attitude if not in our posture), we are acknowledging to God that we are helpless without His working in us. We are acknowledging that to make any progress in our pursuit of holiness, we are absolutely dependent on Him to enlighten our understanding of Scripture and, more important, make it applicable to our lives.

It is often difficult to keep in a right relationship the principles of diligence and dependence. Too frequently, we emphasize one to the relative neglect of the other. In fact, some well-meaning Bible teachers and preachers will deliberately subvert one or the other because of their belief that diligence and dependence are intrinsically incompatible.

The great Puritan pastor and theologian John Owen addressed this misconception in his masterful treatise on the Holy Spirit. Writing of God's promises of grace (in this context, His enabling power), he wrote,

> We need to consider our own duty and the grace of God. Some would separate these things as inconsistent. If holiness be our duty, there is no room for grace; and if it be an effect of grace, there is no place for duty. But our duty and God's grace are nowhere opposed in the matter of sanctification; for the one supposes the other. We cannot perform our duty without the grace of God [i.e., His enabling power], nor does God give us His grace to any other end than that we may rightly perform our duty.[1]

So grace and duty are not incompatible. On the contrary, they are inextricably linked in the dynamics of spiritual transformation.

DILIGENCE AND DEPENDENCE

We see this combination of diligence and dependence in Psalm 119. Though these two principles are scattered throughout the psalm, there are two sections that emphasize them. First, in verses 9-16, the psalmist expressed his diligence:

> How can a young man keep his way pure?
>   By guarding it according to your word.
> With my whole heart I seek you;
>   let me not wander from your commandments!
> I have stored up your word in my heart,
>   that I might not sin against you.
> Blessed are you, O LORD;
>   teach me your statutes!

> With my lips I declare
>> all the rules of your mouth.
> In the way of your testimonies I delight
>> as much as in all riches.
> I will meditate on your precepts
>> and fix my eyes on your ways.
> I will delight in your statutes;
>> I will not forget your word.

Note the personal pronoun *I*, what I do or will do. "I seek you." "I have stored up your word in my heart." "I declare all the rules of your mouth." "In the way of your testimonies I delight." "I will meditate on your precepts." "I will delight in your statutes." "I will not forget your word."

But in verses 33-37, he expressed his dependence:

> Teach me, O LORD, the way of your statutes;
>> and I will keep it to the end.
> Give me understanding, that I may keep your law
>> and observe it with my whole heart.
> Lead me in the path of your commandments,
>> for I delight in it.
> Incline my heart to your testimonies,
>> and not to selfish gain!
> Turn my eyes from looking at worthless things;
>> and give me life in your ways.

Though the pronoun *you* is not used, it is implied all the way through. "O Lord, You teach me." "You give me understanding." "You lead in the path of understanding." "You incline my heart to your testimonies." "You turn my eyes from looking at worthless things." The psalmist was both diligent and dependent.

JONATHAN EDWARDS

One of the finest examples of the relationship of diligence and dependence is in the life of the great early American theologian Jonathan Edwards. Edwards is noted for, among many other things, his seventy resolutions to regulate his heart and life, all written before he was twenty years of age.[2] These resolutions are so severe as to be beyond the comprehension of most present-day Christians. Here are just two examples:

- Resolved, never to do anything, which I should be afraid to do if it were the last hour of my life.
- Resolved, never to give over, nor in the least to slacken, my fight with my corruptions however unsuccessful I may be.

Note the implied diligence in these resolutions. In fact, Edwards reviewed them weekly to keep them fresh in his mind.

But Edwards recognized his dependence on God. Therefore, he prefaced his resolutions with this sentence: "Being sensible that I am unable to do anything without God's help, I do humbly entreat him, by his grace, to enable me to keep the Resolutions, so far as they are agreeable to his will, for Christ's sake."[3]

Yet remarkably, in later years he spoke of too much dependence on his own diligence. Biographer Iain Murray wrote,

Later, while he was far from repudiating the earnestness of those first-days, he came to see more about himself than he had been aware of at the time he penned his resolutions. He had pursued holiness, he subsequently reflected: "with far greater diligence and earnestness than ever I pursued anything in my life, but yet with too great a dependence on my own strength, which afterwards proved a great damage to me. My experience had not then taught me as it has done since, my extreme feebleness and impotence, every manner of way; and the bottomless depths of secret corruption and deceit there was in my heart."[4]

How do we reconcile Edwards' expression of dependence on God penned at the beginning of his resolutions with his confession in later life of too great a dependence on his own strength? While, to my knowledge, he never commented on that, it is reasonable to assume that he progressed from a notional or theoretical awareness of his dependence on God to an actual experiential one as he grew in his Christian walk and saw, as he expressed it, his "extreme feebleness and impotence."

There is a lesson here for all of us today. We can read John 15:4-5 and say, "Yes, that's right. Without Him I can do nothing." We agree with it because it is in the Bible. Jesus said it, so it is true. That's well and good. That's knowledge; that's *ginosko*. But to actually learn to depend on Christ, our theoretical knowledge has to become experiential knowledge. It has to grow from *ginosko* to *epiginosko*. This is characteristic of genuine Christian growth.

I believe this is one reason we so often struggle with our sin. The Holy Spirit withholds His power from us to allow us to experience firsthand the extreme feebleness and impotence Edwards felt. He does this, of course, to draw out from us a sense of desperation so that we, to use the words of Proverbs 2:3, "call out for [help] and raise [our] voice for [His enabling power]."

And when we do fail — and fail we will — in our struggles with our sin, we must go back to the gospel and see Jesus bearing that very sin in His own body on the cross and at the same time clothing us with His righteousness. This unmerited love for us on His part is what gives us the courage and the motivation to press on in the pursuit of holiness, even in the midst of our failure.

FOR GROUP DISCUSSION

1. How would you describe the expression *dependent responsibility* in your own words?
2. How do the Scriptures cited in this chapter in support of the concept of dependent responsibility oppose the theological position that advises, "Let go and let God"?
3. What lesson about the balance between dependence and diligence did Jonathan Edwards learn in his later years? What can we take away from this?

CHAPTER TEN

Instruments of Grace

Be strengthened by the grace that is in Christ Jesus.

2 TIMOTHY 2:1

We have already looked at 2 Timothy 2:1 in chapter 7, where we saw that the grace of Christ by which we are to be strengthened is the power of Christ applied to our lives by the Holy Spirit. But keep in mind that this power is an expression of *grace*, God's blessing through Christ to those who deserve His curse. The power we need to live the Christian life is as much an underserved favor from God as is the gift of our salvation.

In applying the power of Christ to us, however, the Holy Spirit uses means or, as I prefer to call them, instruments of grace. And though they are His instruments, it is our responsibility to take advantage of them. I have a treadmill and a set of weights that I use to try to maintain a reasonable level of physical fitness. These pieces of equipment are instruments of physical fitness, but they will not accomplish their intended purpose if I do not use them. In the same manner, the Holy Spirit's instruments of grace will not accomplish their purpose if I do not take advantage of them. The way we take advantage of them is through what is usually called the practice of spiritual disciplines.

Right away some well-meaning people bristle at the mention of spiritual disciplines. They associate such practices with a spirit of legalism or, as I prefer to call it, a performance attitude. It is true that many of us start out practicing these disciplines because we genuinely want to grow. But over time we gradually slip into a performance mindset toward God in which we think the practice of these disciplines earns God's favor and the failure to practice them earns His disfavor. There is a danger of this attitude creeping into our practice of the disciplines, but we can help avoid that mindset if we think of them as instruments of grace and understand the nature of God's grace as His favor to us through Christ.

Also keep in mind that though the practice of these disciplines involves our activity, we must always depend on the Holy Spirit to make them effective in our lives. As someone has so well said, grace does not make our effort unnecessary but makes it effective. So the same activity is both an instrument of grace from the Holy Spirit and a discipline we practice.

At the same time, we should note that Paul's words "Be strengthened by His grace that is in Christ Jesus" is an imperative. Timothy is to *do* something. He is to be strengthened. True, he cannot strengthen himself, but he can actively draw on the grace that is in Christ, and the means God has given for doing that is through the instruments of grace He has provided.

Now that we have cleared away the underbrush of confusion regarding the relationship of grace and discipline, let's consider the necessity of the spiritual disciplines.

DISCIPLINES

Consider Paul's words to Timothy in 1 Timothy 4:7-8: "Have nothing to do with irreverent, silly myths. Rather train yourself for godliness; for while bodily training is of some value, godliness is of value in every way, as it holds promise for the present life and also for the life to come." The word Paul used that is translated as *train* or *training* was taken from the Greek athletic culture of his day. Originally it referred to the daily training regimen of the athletes as they prepared to participate in the athletic games of that day. Over time it has come to refer to training in any area of life and the discipline associated with that training.

It is a self-evident truth that skill or competency in any area of life is accomplished only by training and discipline. It doesn't matter whether it is the professional areas — such as law, medicine, and engineering — or the mechanical and building trades, or fine arts, or athletics; competence can be developed only through training and discipline. We accept this obvious fact in all temporal areas of life but give little attention to it in the spiritual dimension of our lives.

Yet Paul's words to Timothy — "Train yourself for godliness" (verse 7) — are just as applicable to us today and just as urgent as they were to Timothy. Why? Because as Paul continued in verse 8, "While bodily training is of some value, godliness is of value in every way, as it holds promise for the present life and also for the life to come." Godliness is valuable for both this life and the life to come. No other discipline can make such a claim. When the most brilliant heart surgeon in all the world dies, his skill dies with him. He can't carry it into eternity. The same is true for the world-class concert musician or the top pro athlete. But godliness is valuable for all eternity!

Godliness is basically God-centeredness. It means to live all of life in awareness of our absolute dependence on God and our accountability to Him in both the spiritual and temporal dimensions of life. So it really is at the heart of spiritual transformation. And it is through the practice of the spiritual disciplines that we become more God-centered in our everyday lives.

Any discipline in the temporal realm involves lots of hard work and usually repetitive practice. What is it that keeps a person going in his or her discipline? Obviously, it is the goal of becoming a competent professional, or a skilled craftsman, or a medal-winning athlete.

By contrast, the spiritual disciplines for a Christian should be a source of joy and delight. We should desire to practice them rather than think we "ought" to practice them. Someone once wisely observed that "discipline without desire is drudgery." What is it then that will give us the desire? It is, first of all, the gratitude that grows out of a daily embracing of the gospel. Remember, he who is forgiven much loves much. Second, all of these disciplines in some way involve time with God. Think about what that means! We who are sinful creatures get to spend time with the Creator of the universe, who loved us so much that He sent His Son to live and die in our place. All of us enjoy spending time with someone we love and who loves us. This is the privilege we have in the practice of the spiritual disciplines.

So what are these disciplines or, better, instruments of grace that we should practice?

THE PRIVILEGE OF TIME ALONE WITH GOD

I believe the most important instrument of grace God has given us is the opportunity to spend time with Him each day. This practice is usually called the quiet time or daily devotions, but I prefer to call it time alone with God to emphasize that the goal of this time is not simply to read a chapter or two in the Bible and go through a prayer list. Rather, it is to actually spend time with God through His Word and prayer. What this time alone with God might look like in daily life will be discussed later in this chapter, but for now I want to emphasize the privilege and importance of this practice.

First, consider the privilege. We have seen in earlier chapters that God is the infinitely holy One who hates sin because it is rebellion against His sovereign authority and a despising of His holy character. You and I are still practicing sinners whose very best deeds are, in the eyes of God, no more than a "polluted garment" (Isaiah 64:6). Yet through His Son's sinless life and death on the cross, which God has credited to us, He regards us as righteous and accepts us as His children. He gives us the privilege of addressing Him as "Abba" or "Daddy" or "Dear Father." Think of this! The infinite sovereign and holy Creator of the universe gives us the privilege of entering into an intimate relationship with Himself though we are still practicing sinners every day.

In the earliest chapters of the Bible, we read of a man named Enoch who was the seventh generation from Adam. He was commended by God as one who "walked with God" (see Genesis 5:22-24). The expression "walked with God" is descriptive of a close personal relationship with Him. The fact that the Holy Spirit, who guided the mind of Moses as he wrote Genesis, would single out Enoch from all his ancestors by the expression "He walked with God" indicates to us the importance God attaches to our developing this kind of a relationship with Him. And you and I have the privilege of developing the same kind of relationship with God as Enoch had. In fact, living as we do in the light of God's full revelation in Christ and having at our disposal that revelation in the form of the completed Bible, we have an even greater opportunity and privilege than Enoch did.

Sadly, so few of us take advantage of this privilege. Too often we choose to stay up late at night to watch the ten o'clock news or the late-night television talk shows rather than going to bed at a reasonable hour so we can get up early enough in the morning to spend this time with God. And some who do get up for this time see it more as a duty to earn favor with God or avert His disfavor than the privilege it really is.

I don't want to seem legalistic on this subject by appearing to say that the early-morning hour is the only appropriate time for fellowship with God. I realize some people, such as myself, are "morning people" and others are "night people." But I will say this to those who are "night people." Skip the evening news and the late-night television talk shows and spend that time developing a relationship with God. Why spend time thinking about events that are temporal when you can use that time to think about things that are eternal? (And for those who, because of shift work or being mothers with small children, find neither early morning nor late night suitable, try to find some time during the day when you can have a dedicated amount of time to spend with God.)

Consider Paul's word to the Colossian believers in Colossians 3:1-2: "If then you have been raised with Christ, seek the things that are above, where Christ is, seated at the right hand of God. Set your minds on things that are above, not on things that are on earth." Paul did not write those words to a group of super-spiritual Christians; he wrote them to very ordinary people, many of whom were slaves (see verses 22-24). No, Paul was addressing all of us, regardless of our temporal position in life. He was saying that all of us should "set [our] minds on things that are above, not on things that are on earth." Paul was not trying to lay a guilt trip on these Colossian believers, nor us. No, he was saying, "Think of who you are! You have been raised with Christ. The things of this life are not where you find joy and fulfillment. That comes only in a genuine relationship with God through Christ and by the Holy Spirit. Put your priorities in eternal things."

Let me hasten to point out that time alone with God some-time during the day is not the total fulfillment of what Paul was saying to us in Colossians 3:1-2. Far too many of us can have that dedicated time with God and then go out into our workaday worlds and forget about Him for most of our waking hours. I will address this issue later, but for now let me say that our dedicated time with God provides the foundation for our relationship with Him throughout the day.

This dedicated time with God each day should be the object of our desire, not a duty to perform. Consider the words of the psalmists:

> As a deer pants for flowing streams,
>   so pants my soul for you, O God.

My soul thirsts for God,
  for the living God.
When shall I come and appear before God?
  (Psalm 42:1-2)

O God, you are my God; earnestly I seek you;
  my soul thirsts for you;
my flesh faints for you,
  as in a dry and weary land where there is no water.
  (Psalm 63:1)

Isaiah also said,

My soul yearns for you in the night;
  my spirit within me earnestly seeks you.
For when your judgments are in the earth,
  the inhabitants of the world learn righteousness.
  (Isaiah 26:9)

Do you see the intensity of desire these men had for the opportunity to meet with God? It was not a duty for them; rather, they longed to spend time with God.

The reality for most of us is that we do not experience this longing. For some believers, the idea of spending time with God each day is not even in their thinking. Others will have their quiet time, read a daily Bible reading, say a few prayers, but never really enjoy actual fellowship with God. I suspect that only a small minority of believers experience the longing for and joy of an authentic time with God each day, but this should be the goal of every Christian.

Two questions arise at this point: How do we get this intense desire, and what, on a practical level, does time alone with God look like? Let's try to answer those questions by looking at a suggested structure for this time.

THE GOSPEL

I acknowledge being a rather structured and methodical person, and I realize that many others are more spontaneous and not so structured. So I do not present the following as a "one size fits all" program, but I do believe it is based on solid biblical principles that apply to all of us and can be adapted according to our temperaments and schedules.

I believe our time with God should begin with the gospel, but because the gospel is only for sinners, we start with acknowledging ourselves as still-practicing sinners. I use the tax collector's prayer in Luke 18:13, "God, be merciful to me, a sinner!" I acknowledge that God has already been merciful to me but that I live by His mercy every day. Following this, I review and pray over different gospel Scriptures. My three favorites are Isaiah 53:6, 2 Corinthians 5:21, and Philippians 3:9. Isaiah 53:6 assures me that my sins are forgiven, Philippians 3:9 reminds me that I stand clothed in the righteousness of Christ, and 2 Corinthians 5:21 tells me why both are true.

Dwelling on the gospel, however, should be far more than simply a five- or ten-minute introduction so that we can get on with our Bible reading. It is a significant instrument of grace in its own right that deserves a significant place in our time with God.

We read in 2 Corinthians 3:18, "We all, with unveiled face, beholding the glory of the Lord, are being transformed into the same image from one degree of glory to another. For this comes from the Lord who is the Spirit." As I have already mentioned, this is one of two places in the New Testament where the word *transformed* is used to denote our growth in Christlikeness, the other being Romans 12:2. In both cases, the verb *transformed* is in the passive voice — that is, something is being done *to* us, not *by* us. Yet in both instances, we have a part to play. In Romans 12:2, our part is to bring our minds under the renewing influence of the

Word of God. In 2 Corinthians 3:18, our part is to behold the glory of the Lord. What does that mean?

I believe that the glory of the Lord — that is, of Jesus — is in this context His glory as revealed in the gospel. I say that because in 2 Corinthians 3:7-11, Paul contrasted the glory of the law given by Moses with the far greater glory of the gospel. Then, in 2 Corinthians 4:4, he spoke of "the light of the gospel of the glory of Christ," and in verse 6, he wrote of "the light of the knowledge of the glory of God in the face of Jesus Christ."

Philip Hughes, in his commentary on 2 Corinthians, wrote, "To gaze by faith into the gospel is to behold Christi.... And to contemplate Him who is the Father's image is progressively to be transformed into that image."[1]

In the same vein, John Calvin wrote, "[Paul] declares that through the gospel, with uncovered face and no veil intervening, we behold God's glory with such an effect that we are transformed into His very likeness."[2]

Christ is glorious in all His attributes as the eternal Son of God, but it is His glory as revealed in the gospel that is preeminently in view in this Scripture. So as we behold the glory of the Lord as reflected in the gospel, the Holy Spirit uses the gospel as one of His transforming instruments.

How does this work? For one thing, the gospel frees us up to honestly face our sins and our sinfulness. If we believe we are in a performance-based relationship with God, we will either live in denial about our sin or live under a continual sense of guilt. In the former instance, we see no need for change. In the latter, we will not experience the motivation to change that the gospel brings.

And then, as I developed more extensively in chapter 6, the love of Christ for us as revealed in the gospel will help us want to change for the right reason. God wants us to desire to do what is our duty to do, and only the gospel will produce that desire.

Finally, it is through the gospel that the Holy Spirit testifies to our adoption as God's children. Apart from the gospel, we view

God as our judge rather than as our heavenly Father. And when we view Him as our judge, we tend to obey, to whatever extent we do, out of fear rather than out of love. And we will never be transformed as long as we live by fear instead of love.

The important role of the gospel in our spiritual transformation is not an idea that has been developed in the last twenty to thirty years. In the annals of church history, I have traced it back as far as John Calvin in the sixteenth century. We have read John Owen's words in the seventeenth century (see chapter 5). Consider these from the eighteenth and nineteenth centuries:

> Before we go farther, we have full occasion to observe, of how great importance it is, to preach the special doctrine of the gospel, the doctrine of faith; and that, not only in order to give sinners encouragement respecting free justification, but also with regard to sanctification. The gospel, the doctrine of faith is a special truth of God, and of divine revelation; this is the great means of sanctification, according to that declaration and petition of our blessed Savior to His Father; sanctify them through Thy truth; Thy word is truth.[3]
>
> JAMES FRASER (EIGHTEENTH CENTURY)

> It was "The truth as it is in Jesus" that was the means of our conversion and it is the same truth that is the instrument of our progressive sanctification; for Christ's prayer for His disciples, even when He spoke of the promise of the Spirit, was "Sanctify them through Thy truth; Thy word is truth." And the truth here spoken of is not solely, nor seen chiefly, the truth contained in the law, although that is useful, as affording a perfect rule and authoritative directory for the conduct of life, but it is especially the truth contained in the Gospel; for that affords the most constraining motives to a life of new obedience; and what

"the law cannot do, seeing that it is weak through the flesh," the Gospel can accomplish, because it is, in the hand of the Spirit, an effectual means of sanctification.[4]

JAMES BUCHANAN (NINETEENTH CENTURY)

So don't give the gospel short shrift in your time alone with God. Take time to reflect on it, to enjoy its exhilarating influence on your mind, and then in gratitude to God for His grace and mercy, through Christ, present your body to Him as a living sacrifice.

Now we are ready for Bible reading and prayer.

FOR GROUP DISCUSSION

1. Why should we be diligent to practice the spiritual disciplines?
2. If after reading this chapter you are inclined to make a renewed commitment to spending time alone with God, what is your motivation for doing so? What can you do to help that motivation thrive long term?
3. Describe three ways the Holy Spirit uses the gospel as one of His transforming instruments. How does this differ from a duty or performance-based approach to transformation?

CHAPTER ELEVEN

The Word of God and Prayer

Open my eyes, that I may behold wondrous things out of your law.

PSALM 119:18

T he pastor of the church where I was a member during my
college days read the Bible through four times a year at the
rate of about ten chapters a day, and he was one of the most godly
men I've ever met. I'm not advocating reading ten chapters a day
for the rest of us, but there is a direct correlation between consistent daily Bible reading and our spiritual transformation. For
most of us, that regular Bible reading occurs during our time with
God.

The truth is that all the instruments of grace, in one way or
another, center around the Word of God. This should not sur-
prise us since the Holy Spirit is the agent of transformation and
also the ultimate author of Scripture. The Scriptures, then, are
His chief instruments of His transforming work in us, so careful
and prayerful reading of Scripture should also be a major part of
our time with God.

Again, the only two places in the Bible where the word
transformed is used are Romans 12:2 and 2 Corinthians 3:18. In
Romans 12:2, Paul wrote, "Be transformed by the renewal of

131

your mind." Though the Word of God is not mentioned, it is obviously implied. There is no other way for our minds to be renewed than by exposure to the Word of God. Note that the encouragement to be transformed is set in opposition to being conformed to the world. These are the only two alternatives. There is no neutral third option. We will either be transformed by the renewal of our minds through consistent exposure to Scripture, or we will, by default, be conformed to the values of the world around us. We see this either/or contrast expressed more fully in Psalm 1:1-2:

> Blessed is the man
>> who walks not in the counsel of the wicked,
> nor stands in the way of sinners,
>> nor sits in the seat of scoffers;
> but his delight is in the law of the LORD,
>> and on his law he meditates day and night.

In this Scripture, the psalmist set before us two opposite directions and results. In verse 1, he described a person who is being drawn progressively into the web of sinful society around him or her. In verse 2, he described the person who is being renewed in his mind through delight in and meditation on the Word of God. Don't let the word *meditation* put you off as if it is some mystical practice. Biblical meditation simply means to prayerfully and carefully reflect on Scripture in order to determine what God is saying and the possible application of that Scripture to you.

Returning to Romans 12:2, we see that Paul uses an unusual grammatical structure: a passive imperative. He tells us to be transformed. Why does he use an imperative when he knows we cannot transform ourselves? The answer is that though we cannot transform ourselves, we can and must bring our minds under the continual influence of the Word of God. As we do that, the Holy Spirit will use His Word to do His transforming work in us.

BIBLE READING

So the second part of our time alone with God should be Bible reading. Bible reading is best done according to a plan rather than by simply opening the Bible at random. There are several different Bible-reading schedules available, or you can make up your own. Whatever plan one chooses, I believe that every Christian should read the Scriptures daily. In anticipation that the nation of Israel would want a king, God said of him,

> When he sits on the throne of his kingdom, he shall write for himself in a book a copy of this law, approved by the Levitical priests. And it shall be with him, and he shall read in it all the days of his life, that he may learn to fear the LORD his God by keeping all the words of this law and these statutes, and doing them. (Deuteronomy 17:18-19)

The principle of consistent daily Bible reading and application of what we read that is embedded in these instructions for the king are applicable to us today. Our minds will not be renewed by exposing them to only one thirty- or forty-minute sermon a week. If we are going to be transformed through the renewing of our minds, we need daily exposure to God's Word through daily Bible reading.

Keep in mind that the object of our Bible reading is not to grow in merely an intellectual grasp of biblical truth but to listen to Him as He speaks to us through His Word. Remember that regardless of who the human author is of the passage we are reading, it is ultimately the Holy Spirit who is speaking to us. What the text says, He says.

As we open our Bibles to read, we should do so with a prayer that God, through His Spirit, will meet with us in His Word. In 2 Timothy 3:16, Paul said that all Scripture is "profitable for teaching, for reproof, for correction, and for training in righteousness."

I pray over that verse (adding, "and encouragement"), asking that God will teach, rebuke, correct, and encourage me in whatever way He knows I need. That is to say I am not looking merely for intellectual information; I want God to teach me more about Himself and to address specific issues in my life.

Sometimes the Scripture I am reading is very direct, such as "Do not be anxious about anything" (Philippians 4:6) and God speaks to me about my tendency to anxiety in some particular situation. At another time, He may use a principle from a totally unrelated situation to address an issue in my life. Once God used Paul's words "We worked night and day" (1 Thessalonians 2:9) to rebuke me for feeling sorry for myself because I was working into the evening every day just to keep up with my ministry responsibilities.

I don't want to give the impression that I get some great insight or great instruction from God every day as I read my Bible. Sometimes I receive nothing at all. God is sovereign and infinitely wise. He knows what we need, and He apportions to us the truth He knows we need as we need it. But if we will humbly and expectantly look to Him, He will teach us and train us as He sees fit. After all, He is the agent of our spiritual transformation. He is far more desirous that we profit from our Bible reading than we are.

PRAYER

The third major element of our time alone with God is prayer. First, we should pray as we read our Bibles. The nature of our prayer will vary depending on what we are reading. Sometimes we will want to pray for understanding of the text. At other times, it might be a prayer of thanksgiving or the confession of sin revealed or for the enabling power of the Spirit to deal with the sin exposed. Sometimes it might be a prayer of appropriating some promise in the text or a cry for the faith to even believe the promise. Whatever the appropriate response is, we should pray as we read. The idea of praying as we read implies that we should read thoughtfully and reflectively. This may seem self-evident to some, but I do not want to take it for granted that everyone sees this. So read, reflect, and pray over what you are reading.

Second, we should not only pray as we read our Bible but we should have a period of time dedicated to just prayer. The Bible is full of the subject of prayer, and scores of books have been written about it, so it is beyond the scope of this book to address prayer as a broad subject. Instead, I want to focus on prayer that I believe is particularly pertinent to our time with God and then look at prayer as an instrument of grace for our spiritual transformation.

Our time with God is not about "me"; it is primarily about God — His glory and His will. And the one passage of Scripture on prayer that focuses on God's glory and God's will is the Lord's Prayer, recorded in Matthew 6:9-13:

Our Father in heaven, hallowed be your name. Your king-dom come, your will be done, on earth as it is in heaven. Give us this day our daily bread, and forgive us our debts, as we also have forgiven our debtors. And lead us not into temptation, but deliver us from evil.

As we look at this prayer, we see that it easily divides into two parts. The first focuses on God (see verses 9-10) and the latter on our needs, both temporal and spiritual (see verses 11-13). The fact that Jesus puts God's glory and God's will before our needs should tell us something: If we want our time with God to be in fact a time with God, we should put His glory and His will above our needs. But if most of us will examine our quiet-time prayers, we will discover that our prayers lie mostly in the second part of the Lord's Prayer. We pray more about our needs, both temporal and spiritual (but probably more in the temporal area), than we do about God's glory and will.

Therefore, in our time with God, it is good to expand our horizons beyond ourselves and our families and consider the work of God worldwide. The way God's name will be hallowed, His kingdom come (at least in this age), and His will be done is through the proclamation of the gospel so that people trust Jesus as Savior and obey Him as Lord. In the spirit of Acts 1:8 (Jerusalem, Judea, Samaria, and the ends of the earth), we should pray for the spread of the gospel in our local church (or campus or military base ministry), in our community, in our nation, and to the ends of the earth. Does your prayer during your time with God reflect this interest in His glory and will?

As we come to the second part of the Lord's Prayer, we notice that it includes both daily needs (I believe that "our daily bread" stands for all our physical and material needs) and spiritual needs. Again, I suspect that most of us give the majority of our prayer time to our temporal needs. It is not wrong to pray for these needs. Jesus instructs us to do so. After all, prayer for those needs is (or should be) an acknowledgment that all we have in this life is a gift from God our Father. It is an acknowledgment that we are dependent on Him for everything.

But we are also to pray for our spiritual needs, and it is here that we see prayer as an instrument of grace that God has provided for our spiritual transformation. We know that we are both responsible and dependent, and prayer is, among other things, an expression of that dependence. It is an acknowledgment that we are helpless in ourselves — that we are dependent on the Holy Spirit to both do His own work and enable us to do the work we must do.

As we bring our minds under the influence of Scripture, the Holy Spirit will begin to reveal to us areas of our lives that need to be transformed. Sometimes it will be a sinful attitude or action that needs to be "put to death" (Romans 8:13). At other times, He will make us aware of character traits that Paul called the fruit of the Spirit (see Galatians 5:22-23) in which we need to grow. As we become aware of these areas, we need to pray specifically for the work of the Holy Spirit to both change us and enable us to change. I find it helpful to keep a private list of sin patterns I need to "put to death" and of positive traits in which I see a need to grow. I always try to associate one or more appropriate Scriptures with each area of need and pray over those Scriptures.

For example, I am to love my wife as Christ loves the church (see Ephesians 5:25). Because this is an area in which I will never perfectly "arrive," I keep that subject on my prayer list along with the Scripture reference to remind myself to pray about this daily. In this age where sex is magnified, the lingering look is always a temptation for men, so I pray the first part of Psalm 119:37, "Turn my eyes from looking at worthless things."

I also pray that I will be motivated to obey and serve Christ out of love and gratitude, not out of a sense of duty. In this connection, I ask God to give me the same sense of love and devotion the sinful woman had when she anointed the feet of Jesus (see Luke 7:36-50 and my discussion of it in chapter 6). As I read the Scriptures, I pray that the Holy Spirit will bring to my mind areas of my life that need to be changed and then that He will work in me both "to will and to work" (Philippians 2:13). We are to "be doers of the word, and not hearers [or readers] only" (James 1:22), and the doing always begins with prayer for the direction and help of the Holy Spirit. Keep in mind that prayer for spiritual transformation is both a duty and a privilege. It is an instrument of grace God has provided, but it is also a spiritual discipline we must practice if we are to be progressively transformed. Also, keep in mind that prayer for transformation does not yield quick results. Growth in "putting off" and "putting on" comes over time.

Lastly, in my time alone with God, I pray for family and friends. For our children and their spouses I pray, first of all, for their spiritual lives. I pray that they will be "taught by the LORD" (Isaiah 54:13) and that God will work in them "that which is pleasing in his sight" (Hebrews 13:21). Then I pray about more temporal needs they have, including the jobs of both our son and son-in-law. I pray that all of our grandchildren (and I mention each one by name) will come to trust Christ as Savior and obey and serve Him as Lord.

I pray for a small group of friends, for both their spiritual and temporal needs as I become aware of them. (If you do this and your list becomes too long and burdensome, you might consider putting them on a one-day-a-week rotating basis: Bob on Monday, Joe on Tuesday, Sam on Wednesday, and so on.)

Lest I appear to be a spiritual giant in prayer, let me acknowledge that this is the spiritual discipline in which I struggle most to be fresh and motivated. I readily identify with someone who said, "We hardly begin to pray and we are done." More than that, however, is the tendency to just go down the list of people and their needs without a heart for what I'm doing. But Paul said the Spirit helps us in our weakness. He will give us the desire and motivation to pray if we ask Him. God urges us to pray and promises to hear our prayers, so we should make genuine fervent prayer a part of our time alone with Him.

The gospel, the Scriptures, and prayer — these are the major components of our time alone with God. There are other instruments of grace God has provided for us, thus disciplines we should practice, and to these we will turn next.

MEMORIZATION AND MEDITATION

While I believe that our time alone with God is the foundational spiritual discipline, there are others we should also practice. Whereas time alone with God is a focused, concentrated time at some point in our day, these other disciplines can and should be practiced to some degree throughout the day.

Scripture memorization is probably the most important of these daily disciplines and is indeed an instrument of God's grace. I have been using memorized Scripture in my life for sixty years, and nothing has paid greater dividends for the time spent than this discipline. I cannot count for even one month the number of times the Holy Spirit has brought to mind a memorized verse to warn me against temptation, guide in decision making, encourage me in a time of stress or anxiety, and help me with countless other situations I encounter in the course of a day.

This discipline must surely be what the psalmist had in mind when he wrote, "I have stored up your word in my heart, that I might not sin against you" (Psalm 119:11). The purpose of storing up anything is to meet some anticipated future need. When we set aside present income for future retirement needs, we are in effect storing up money to be used in the time when we may not have a current income. Though the practice seems to have largely disappeared, during my childhood many homemakers canned fruits and vegetables in the summer to be eaten in the winter. They were storing up food to be eaten at a later time.

As far as Scripture memorization is concerned, the most notable example of storing up is in the life of Jesus. When the Devil tempted him during His forty days in the wilderness, He answered each temptation from Scripture (see Matthew 4:1-10). As a child, Jesus had stored up God's Word in His heart so that when Satan tempted Him, He was able to respond from Scripture. Jesus frequently quoted Scripture on other occasions, so it is obvious that He had memorized vast amounts of it. And the fact that Jesus used memorized Scripture to respond to temptations surely sets an example for us to follow.

Of course, we need to memorize more than the commands of Scripture. If we are going to "preach the gospel to ourselves" each day, we need to memorize key gospel verses. It is also valuable to memorize some of the promises of Scripture. Consider how these words of Hebrews 13:5, "I will never leave you nor forsake you," can encourage you and enable you to trust God in a stressful situation. And that is just one of many promises you can store up for a time when you need to trust in the sovereignty and goodness of God.

However, we need to do more than store up God's Word in our hearts; in the words of Psalm 1:2, we need to "[meditate on it] day and night." The expression *day and night* is an idiom for consistently or regularly. It should be our daily practice to meditate on Scripture. And again, the word *meditate* in the Bible simply means to reflect on or ponder over a passage of Scripture and make application to our lives, whether the Scripture be about God, the gospel, a command, or a promise. We need all of them if we are to be progressively transformed into the image of Christ. One of the advantages of Scripture memorization is that we have verses in our minds that we can meditate on during the course of the day.

HEARING THE WORD

The most common instrument of grace God uses is our opportunity to worship together and hear the Word of God taught in our local churches. Though this means is considered by some to be of little lasting value, we should remember that until the invention of the printing press in the fifteenth century, this was the only means of exposure to Scripture for most people. Even today with our proliferation of small-group Bible studies, hearing the Word taught in our churches is the most common means of exposure to God's Word.

Why is it of not more lasting effect? While lack of effective teaching may often be the cause, I believe the greater problem is lack of effective hearing. Thousands of people come to our evangelical churches each Sunday to enjoy the sermon without expecting any life change from what they hear. They are like the Jewish people of Ezekiel's day of whom God said, "They come to you as people come, and they sit before you as my people, and they hear what you say but they will not do it" (Ezekiel 33:31). Remember the distinction between *ginosko*, intellectual knowledge, and *espiginosko*, the knowledge applied and experienced in one's life. Too often our hearing the Scriptures results at best in a *ginosko* grasp of truth, so we should come prayerfully to hear God's Word taught so that we may apply what we hear.

Some people today would write off the local church and its preaching and teaching ministry as ineffective and out of date in this age of rapidly changing means of communication. But the message of the Bible does not change in response to changing culture and technology, and it is clear from the New Testament that God's people met together for worship and hearing the Word of God taught (see, for example, Acts 2:42; 20:7; Romans 16:5; 1 Timothy 4:13; 2 Timothy 4:1-2; Hebrews 10:24-25).

Worshipping together regularly also provides the opportunity to partake of the Lord's Supper with fellow believers. That this was a regular practice of first-century churches seems clear from Paul's instruction concerning it and his rebuke for improper observance by the Corinthian church (see 1 Corinthians 11:17-34). Though many of us may observe the Lord's Supper in a reverent but perfunctory manner, it is indeed an instrument of grace that God has provided. As we silently wait for the elements to be distributed, we should use that time to reflect on and thank the Lord for His sacrifice for our sins. By that action, we are beholding the glory of the Lord in the gospel (see 2 Corinthians 3:18), and the Spirit of God will use it as a transforming instrument in our lives.

Somewhat akin to hearing the Bible taught is the reading of Christian books, in that we benefit from the teaching of others. There are many varieties of Christian books and varying degrees of helpfulness. Some merely express the author's own ideas, which may or may not be based on Scripture. The best books, in my opinion, are those based solidly on Scripture and draw the reader back to the Scriptures. Once again, however, even a good book based on Scripture is only as beneficial as the application we make from it.

Whether it's hearing the Word preached or taught or reading a Christian book, we should all be like the Bereans, who received the Word taught with all eagerness but then examined the Scriptures daily to see if what Paul taught was true (see Acts 17:11). The fact is that we have many excellent oral communicators and writers who can make a persuasive message and convince us by their rhetorical or writing skills. A friend said of one such speaker, "He is one of the most persuasive speakers I have ever heard but one of the most dangerous." He was dangerous because he was a skillful communicator with a growing influence on others but was not teaching the truth. So we should follow the example of the Bereans to examine what we hear by the Word of God.

PRAYER THROUGHOUT THE DAY

We have already looked at prayer as a part of our time alone with God, but Paul instructed us to "pray without ceasing" (1 Thessalonians 5:17). "Without ceasing" simply means regularly and continually. It is somewhat akin to the "day and night" idiom of Psalm 1:2. The application of both of these instructions is that we should make it a practice throughout the day to think about Scripture and pray. In this way, we can have fellowship with God not only at a specified time but many times a day.

Many people work at jobs that require mental concentration and obviously cannot meditate on Scripture or pray throughout the day. But consider this: When you can think of anything you want to think about, what do you think about? Do you make any effort to "set your minds on things that are above, not on things that are on earth" (Colossians 3:2)? Are you taking advantage of the instruments of grace that God has provided?

There are many occasions to pray throughout the day. We should pray for safety as we drive, we should pray that God will keep us from temptations to sin, we should pray that we will be a testimony to the gospel in our work and that our children will be protected mentally, physically, and spiritually while in school. These are just examples of how we might pray throughout the day.

Remember, all these spiritual activities are the Holy Spirit's instruments of grace. Taking advantage of them as disciplines will not earn us favor with God, but just as a musician or athlete cannot achieve any measure of competence or skill without the discipline of practice, so we cannot attain any level of spiritual maturity if we do not see these disciplines as expressions of God's grace and delight in the use of them. Don't set desire and duty in opposition to one another, but pray that through the motivation of the gospel the Holy Spirit will give you the desire to do your duty.

FOR GROUP DISCUSSION

1. What are the three major elements of our daily time alone with God?
2. What does meditating on Scripture consist of and why is it important?
3. With the exception of our daily time alone with God, Scripture memorization is probably the most important spiritual discipline (instrument of grace). Why?

CHAPTER TWELVE

The Grace of Adversity

You know that the testing of your faith produces steadfastness.
And let steadfastness have its full effect, that you may be
perfect and complete, lacking in nothing.

JAMES 1:3-4

"The grace of adversity" sounds like an oxymoron — a contradiction in terms. If grace is God's blessings through Christ, how can we say that adversity of any kind is a blessing? The answer is in the above passage of James, stating that trials ultimately produce maturity of character. Paul wrote similarly in Romans 5:3-4 that suffering produces endurance, and endurance produces character. The blessing then is not in the circumstance of adversity considered in itself but in the fact that the Holy Spirit is using that adversity to produce more Christlike character in our lives.

Paul wrote in Romans 8:28, "We know that for those who love God all things work together for good, for those who are called according to his purpose." This verse must be understood to say that God causes all things (that is, all events and circumstances in our lives) to work together for good, with the good clarified in verse 29 as conformity to the image of God's Son. And one of the instruments of grace that the Holy Spirit uses is the instrument of adversity.

The fact that God uses all events and circumstances necessarily assumes that God controls and directs all the circumstances of our lives. Actually, God controls and directs all events and circumstances in His entire universe. This truth is known as the providence of God, and it assumes the sovereignty of God over everything in both the spiritual and physical realms. It also assumes His constant involvement in all circumstances and events. The proof of this is beyond the scope of this book, but consider just two Scriptures, Matthew 10:29-31 and Luke 12:6-7. God controls the destiny of a single sparrow and He never forgets one! If this is true of a sparrow, how much more is it true of us.[1]

It is clear then that providential, or God-orchestrated, circumstances are some of the Holy Spirit's instruments of our spiritual transformation. But how can they be disciplines we must practice? The answer is in our response to them. Remember, the spiritual disciplines are activities (or, in this case, quite often attitudinal responses) through which we train ourselves toward holiness. Therefore, we should work at training ourselves to respond to all circumstances and events in a biblical manner. What might this look like in everyday life? The most thorough and helpful treatment of this subject is Hebrews 12:4-11, and to this we will now turn:

> In your struggle against sin you have not yet resisted to the point of shedding your blood. And have you forgotten the exhortation that addresses you as sons?
>
> > "My son, do not regard lightly the discipline of the Lord,
> >   nor be weary when reproved by him.
> > For the Lord disciplines the one he loves,
> >   and chastises every son whom he receives."
>
> It is for discipline that you have to endure. God is treating you as sons. For what son is there whom his father does not discipline? If you are left without discipline, in

which all have participated, then you are illegitimate children and not sons. Besides this, we have had earthly fathers who disciplined us and we respected them. Shall we not much more be subject to the Father of spirits and live? For they disciplined us for a short time as it seemed best to them, but he disciplines us for our good, that we may share his holiness. For the moment all discipline seems painful rather than pleasant, but later it yields the peaceful fruit of righteousness to those who have been trained by it.

The writer of Hebrews spoke of the discipline of the Lord. The word *discipline* as used here does not refer to punishment but rather to child training. Paul used the same word in Ephesians 6:4, "Fathers, do not provoke your children to anger, but bring them up in the discipline and instruction of the Lord." There is no indication in the book of Hebrews that the recipients of this letter were involved in some form of disobedience; rather, they were undergoing significant trials or adversity for being followers of Jesus (see, for example, Hebrews 10:32-34). So the particular expression of God's discipline or child training in this passage is adversity, and the writer wanted his readers to understand both the purpose of the adversity and the biblical response to it.

THE FACT OF ADVERSITY

The first truth we see in the Hebrews passage is the fact of adversity: "The Lord disciplines the one he loves" (12:6). We should not be surprised at this. The psalmist experienced it (see Psalm 119:67,71), Jesus forewarned His disciples about it (see John 15:18-21; 16:1-4,33), Paul frequently spoke of it (see Romans 5:3-5; 8:18,31,37-39; 2 Corinthians 4:16-18), and it is a major subject in Peter's first letter (see 1 Peter 1:6-7; 2:18-21; 3:14-17; 4:1-2,12-19).

The source of adversity in most of the passages cited above is the mistreatment by unbelievers of those who follow Christ, and of course this is a fact of life in many parts of the world today. Even in the West, where we have seldom suffered official persecution, many believers face discrimination or marginalization in the workplace or ridicule in the classroom or misunderstanding from family and friends.

But adversity comes in many forms. It can be a physical disability or chronic illness, the death of a loved one, the disappointing behavior of a spouse, the alienation of parents or children, or many other circumstances too numerous to list. To use a newspaper analogy, some of them make the headlines of our lives, while others lie buried in the inside pages of our hearts and are known only to ourselves. But whatever the nature and extent of the adversity, it is under the sovereign and loving control of our Father. In fact, the writer of Hebrews was quite clear that the Lord disciplines the one He loves, so adversity is not the mark of an uncaring or angry God; rather, it is one proof of His love for us.

THE PURPOSE OF ADVERSITY

The writer of Hebrews stated that God "disciplines us for our good, that we may share in his holiness" (12:10). To share in His holiness is the same as being conformed to the image of Christ, so God disciplines us through adversity to make us more like Christ.

I have previously said that God's Word is the primary instrument the Holy Spirit uses in our transformation process. But it is in the crucible of adversity that Christian character traits are most often developed. For example, the Bible teaches us that we are to love one another. But we actually learn more of what it means to love someone when that someone is difficult to love. There is an old saying, "To love the whole world for me is no chore. My only problem is my neighbor next door." The "neighbor" may be anyone difficult to love whom God has placed in our lives, and in that situation we learn that we cannot just decide that we will love the person; we learn experientially that we are dependent on the Holy Spirit to change us and enable us to love.

The same principle applies in such godly traits as meekness and patience. We learn from the Bible that we are to "put them on" (see Colossians 3:12). But then the Holy Spirit brings into our lives people who will mistreat us or try our patience. Once again we are driven to the Spirit to work in our hearts to change us and enable us to respond with meekness to mistreatment or exercise patience toward someone whose actions arouse feelings of impatience in our hearts.

The purpose of adversity is often illustrated by a caterpillar struggling to break out of its cocoon into a beautiful butterfly. Watching such a struggle, we might want to help the butterfly by snipping open the cocoon. But the struggle to emerge is necessary for developing the muscle system and pushing the body fluids into the wings to expand them. And it is the trials of various kinds that produce the fruit of Christlike character. So much of the time, however, we pray that God will snip open the "cocoon" of our adversity, but God will not do it because He loves us and aims for the result the adversity will produce.

OUR RESPONSE TO ADVERSITY

Given the fact of adversity in our lives and God's purpose for it, how should we respond to it? The writer of Hebrews said we should submit to it, knowing that our Father disciplines us for our good that we may share His holiness (see 12:9-10). Peter wrote that we should humble ourselves under the mighty hand of God, looking to Him for the grace — that is, the divine enablement — to do it (see 1 Peter 5:5-6). We can either chafe under adversity or submit to it. And even in submission, we can do so reluctantly because we have no choice or we can accept it, believing that our infinitely wise and loving heavenly Father has a good and beneficial purpose for it. Therefore, we should pray for the enabling grace to trust in the goodness and wisdom of God, and we should store up Scripture in our hearts to help us do this.

The prophet Jeremiah exercised his ministry during the most difficult and tragic days in Judah's history: the destruction of Jerusalem and the exile of most of its people to faraway Babylon. At some point in this terrible time, Jeremiah wrote Lamentations. Consider his words:

> Remember my affliction and my wanderings,
>   the wormwood and the gall!
> My soul continually remembers it
>   and is bowed down within me.
> But this I call to mind,
>   and therefore I have hope:
>
> The steadfast love of the LORD never ceases;
>   his mercies never come to an end;
> they are new every morning;
>   great is your faithfulness.
> "The LORD is my portion," says my soul,
>   "therefore I will hope in him." (3:19-24)

Notice the change from his attitude of despondency in the first two sentences to one of hope and trust. What caused the change? It was calling to mind the steadfast love and never-ending mercies of the Lord. We need to be like Jeremiah. We need to believe that the discipline of the Father's "mighty hand" is exercised by the One whose love is steadfast and whose mercies never come to an end. In order to believe these truths, however, we need to store up such Scriptures as 1 Peter 5:5-6 and Lamentations 3:22-23 and then ask the Holy Spirit for the grace to believe them.

Some years ago, my wife and I found ourselves in a difficult predicament. As I tried several ways to get out of the situation, the Spirit of God brought to my mind the words of Ecclesiastes 7:13, "Consider the work of God: who can make straight what he has made crooked?" It seemed as if God was saying to me, "This is My doing. You cannot make straight what I have made crooked." But at the same time, the Spirit brought to my mind the words "I will never leave you nor forsake you" (Hebrews 13:5). God did deliver us in that situation, and since then, Hebrews 13:5 has been a rock of confidence for me.

My wife's and my experience was certainly minor compared to Jeremiah's, but in both cases the Word of God was brought to bear on the difficult circumstance. This is another way we should respond to adversity; we should always bring Scripture to bear on it.

On another occasion when I was still a young Christian, I felt that God had not come through for me as I expected Him to. I did not have much Scripture stored up at that time, so the Spirit providentially directed my attention to Job 34:18-19 in the King James Version (the only version you will find this rendering in): "Is it fit to say to a king, Thou art wicked? and to princes, Ye are ungodly? How much less to him that accepteth not the persons of princes, nor regardeth the rich more than the poor? for they all are the work of his hands."

The message of rebuke was clear. If we should not accuse a king of wickedness, how much less should we accuse God of being unfaithful. I was stunned. I was deeply convicted of my arrogance of accusing God of not being fair to me. I fell on my knees and confessed my sin to God.

I learned a valuable lesson that day. The providentially ordained adversity combined with the providential direction of me to Job 34:18-19 had a twofold effect. It convicted me of my sinful, arrogant accusatory attitude toward God, and it also taught me the importance of having the Word of God stored up in my heart so that I (or the Holy Spirit) could bring it to mind at a needful time.

Some years later, the Holy Spirit used another verse from Job to deal with a very painful circumstance, but this time the verse was stored up in my mind. The painful event occurred on a Thursday afternoon and I was scheduled to speak at a local conference beginning Friday evening. How could I do that when I had been totally devastated? Friday morning I awakened with Job 1:21 going through my mind: "He said, 'Naked I came from my mother's womb, and naked shall I return. The LORD gave, and the LORD has taken away; blessed be the name of the LORD.'"

I knelt at our living room couch and said, "Father, You gave and You have taken away. Blessed be Your name." With that my turbulent emotions were stilled and I went to the conference that evening as if nothing had happened.

In that instance, the Holy Spirit brought to my mind the appropriate Scripture, one that I had stored up years before. The principle of storing up God's Word in our hearts applies not only as a defense against temptation but also as a means of responding to any life situation and, in the context of this chapter, particularly as a means of coping with adversity.

But I must hasten to add that it is not just memorizing certain verses that will enable us to cope; those Scriptures must be applied to our hearts by the Holy Spirit. Sometimes He will bring them to our minds and enable us to apply them, as He did for me with Job 1:21. At other times, we may have to comb through our mental file of stored-up verses to find an appropriate Scripture. And when we find one, we must ask the Spirit to apply it to our situation. The bare Scripture by itself is of no avail apart from the Spirit's applying it to our hearts.

THE FRUIT OF ADVERSITY

We should keep in mind that the primary purpose of adversity is growth in our character. This is expressed in Hebrews 12:10-11 as sharing God's holiness and experiencing the peaceful fruit of righteousness. Paul said that our adversity produces character (see Romans 5:3-4), and James said the trials of adversity ultimately produce mature character (see 1:3). It is important that we realize that God's primary objective in the adversities we face is growth in our character — that is, in increased conformity to the likeness of Christ. It may and often does result in some increase or more fruitfulness in ministry, but this is a by-product of our maturing in character.

One of the areas most of us need to grow in is an increasing sense of our dependence on God. Our culture worships self-reliance and self-sufficiency. Speakers at motivational seminars will tell us, "You can do anything you want if you just believe in yourself." Teachers and coaches will say something such as, "You can do it if you just set your mind to it and work at it."

But consider the apostle Paul. Concerning a particular experience, he wrote,

> We do not want you to be ignorant, brothers, of the affliction we experienced in Asia. For we were so utterly burdened beyond our strength that we despaired of life itself. Indeed, we felt that we had received the sentence of death. But that was to make us rely not on ourselves but on God who raises the dead. (2 Corinthians 1:8-9)

Note that Paul said that experience was to make him rely not on himself but on God. Paul was undoubtedly the most gifted and capable of all the apostles, yet God brought such adversity into his life that he was forced to rely entirely on God. God will often do the same for us. In fact, He will sometimes blight the area we feel most confident in so that we will learn to depend on Him, not on ourselves.

Several years prior to his near-death experience, Paul had an altogether different experience: He was caught up into paradise, into the very presence of God, and heard things that could not be repeated (see 2 Corinthians 12:1-10). To curb any temptation to pride over this experience, God gave Paul what he called "a thorn in the flesh." Paul does not tell us the nature of this "thorn," and it is vain to speculate as to what it was, but whatever the nature of this thorn, Paul pleaded with God three times for its removal. God's answer to Paul was, "My grace is sufficient for you, for my power is made perfect in weakness" (verse 9).

Though this promise was given to Paul, it is a universal truth that should be appropriated by all of us. The grace of God's power is displayed most in our own weakness. The problem is that we don't like weakness. We want to be strong, and we want to be in control. Paul, however, gloried in his weakness, because as he said, "When I am weak, then I am strong" (verse 10).

The question we must answer for ourselves then is this: Am I willing to be weak in myself in order that I might experience the power of God in my life? I was born with a body that is less than normal, and advancing years have only made those abnormalities more pronounced. Almost daily I think of Paul's words in 2 Corinthians 4:7, "We have this treasure in jars of clay, to show that the surpassing power belongs to God and not to us." And I think to myself, *My jar is becoming gradually more chipped and cracked.*

Then I go back to God and say, "Father, I am Your servant. My body belongs to You. If You want it to be 'chipped and cracked,' that is Your business. But by Your grace, would You display Your power in my weakness?" I have had the privilege of writing over a period of some thirty years about a dozen books, and God has graciously blessed the ministry of all of them. But the three or four that have been most blessed by God in the lives of readers have all been born out of adversity and struggle. God has displayed His power in my weakness.

So "the grace of adversity" is not an oxymoron; it is a biblical principle. Adversity is always a blessing, though it usually comes disguised. Paul wrote in 1 Thessalonians 5:18, "Give thanks in all circumstances; for this is the will of God in Christ Jesus for you." How can I possibly give thanks in *all* circumstances? How can I thank God that my eyesight and hearing, both of which have been subnormal all my life, are now deteriorating even further? The answer is that God is causing all these circumstances to work together for my good, to conform me to the image of His Son. All the adversity we encounter in life is directed to that end, and so adversity truly is an expression of His grace.

FOR GROUP DISCUSSION

1. What can we learn from Jeremiah's response to adversity in Lamentations 3:19-24?
2. Is harboring or expressing anger toward God a biblical response to our adversity? Why or why not?
3. What is the fruit (benefit) of adversity? Will we bear or receive it if we do not respond in a biblical manner to the grace of adversity?

CHAPTER THIRTEEN

Transformed into His Image

I have come down from heaven, not to do my own will but the will of him who sent me.

JOHN 6:38

W e began our studies on spiritual transformation with Paul's words in Romans 8:29 that God has predestined all believers to be conformed to the image of His Son. This purpose of God will ultimately be fulfilled at the return of Christ because, as John said, "we know that when he appears we shall be like him, because we shall see him as he is" (1 John 3:2). Meanwhile, in this life we are progressively being transformed into that image. That's what this book is all about.

THE IMAGE OF CHRIST

But what does that image look like? It looks like Jesus in His humanity as He lived a real life in a real world for thirty-three years. We have already seen in chapter 4 that during those thirty-three years, He lived a sinless, or perfectly obedient, life. He fulfilled the commandments to love God with His whole being and His neighbor as Himself (see Matthew 22:37-39). However, there is something more basic about Jesus that actually underlies His perfect obedience: His relationship with the Father and His desire to please Him and do His will.

Consider John 6:38, the text at the head of this chapter. Jesus said, "I have come ... not to do my own will but the will of him who sent me." Of course Jesus' will was never contrary to the will of His Father. In fact, in John 5:30, He said, "I seek not my own will but the will of him who sent me." And speaking prophetically through David, He said in Psalm 40:8, "I delight to do your will, O my God; your law is within my heart."

Jesus came to do the will of the Father. He actively sought that will, and He delighted in doing it. If we are to be conformed more and more to the image of Christ, the will of God must become the primary object of our lives.

This means we should be seeking to know and understand the moral will of God as it is given to us in His Word. That is why Paul prayed that the Colossians, and by extension every succeeding generation of believers, "may be filled with the knowledge of his will in all spiritual wisdom and understanding" (Colossians 1:9). We should pray this for ourselves and for those for whom we have a spiritual responsibility (such as parents for their children). Additionally, as Psalm 1:2 says, we should delight in the law of the Lord, where the word *law* stands for the moral will of God. To delight in the law of God means more than just to delight to think about it. It obviously includes that, but it also includes delight in *doing* it, just as Jesus did.

But what I want us to see about Jesus as our example is His heart for the will of God — the heart in the very center of our being, the seat of our intellect, affections (or desires), and will. And Jesus' heart was fully set on knowing and doing the will of the Father. If we are to become increasingly like Jesus, we must give attention to the direction of our hearts and to their objects of desire. Jesus said, "Where your treasure is, there your heart will be also" (Matthew 6:21). Though Jesus spoke those words in the context of money and possessions, the principle is true in every area of life. Desires determine the direction of our hearts. All of us have many desires, some significant and some mundane and incidental. Some are sinful desires, and some are legitimate and amoral. Our desires are to some extent our "treasures."

The morning I was to begin working on this chapter, my wife had an early-morning meeting. In her rush to get out of the house, she left undone a couple of small household tasks she would normally do. I noted these two things, but I also was very desirous to get to my work, so what should I have done? Should I have ignored those household tasks, thinking she would do them when she came home? Or should I have sought in a very small way to love my wife as Christ loved the church by doing these incidental household chores for her? Because I pray regularly that the Holy Spirit will enable me to love her as Christ loved the church, I saw this as an opportunity to love my wife in a practical way. My desire to follow the pattern of Jesus in a small way overcame my desire to get to my work.

I realize this mundane event may seem so incidental that it is scarcely worth mentioning. But the fact is, life is made up of a mosaic of seemingly small and incidental events. All day long we are following our desires, and the overall response to those desires ultimately determines the direction of our lives. So if we desire to be conformed more so to the character of Jesus, we must desire to know and do the will of God. This means we must continually bring our minds under the influence of the Scriptures by the various means discussed in chapter 11, and we must pray that the Holy Spirit will use those means to increase our knowledge of the will of God and our desire to do it.

But what will cause us to *want* to do what we *ought* to do? The answer is *gratitude* for what God has done for us in Christ and the love for God that flows out of that gratitude. This is why we must continually embrace the gospel every day of our lives, for he that is forgiven much loves much. It is the love of Christ for us that constrains us to live no longer for ourselves but for Him.

Jesus used two other expressions about His relationship with His Father that will help us know more of what it means to be conformed to His likeness. In John 8:29, He said, "I always do the things that are pleasing to him." And in John 17:4, in His prayer to the Father, He said, "I glorified you on earth." Of course, pleasing God and glorifying God are the results of doing the will of God, but pleasing and glorifying God give us the goal of doing the will of God. If we are constrained by His love, we will want to please Him and glorify Him.

Once again we find in Paul's letters comparable ideas for us as we seek to be like Jesus. We have already looked at Paul's prayer in Colossians 1:9 that we might grow in the knowledge of God's will. In verse 10, he continued, "Walk in a manner worthy of the Lord, fully pleasing to him." And in 1 Corinthians 10:31, he wrote, "Whether you eat or drink, or whatever you do, do all to the glory of God." Just as Jesus did, Paul desired that we please God and glorify Him in every aspect of our lives.

We might ask how we can please God when even our best deeds are imperfect and are defiled by our own, to some degree, impure motives. The answer is found in the words of Peter in 1 Peter 2:5: "You yourselves like living stones are being built up as a spiritual house, to be a holy priesthood, to offer spiritual sacrifices acceptable to God through Jesus Christ." Our efforts at pleasing God are acceptable to Him because of the perfect obedience of Christ. He is the One who takes our imperfect and defiled obedience and makes it acceptable to God the Father.

So in our desire to do the will of God, to please Him and glorify Him, we must always look outside of ourselves to Christ. We must look to Him for our righteous standing before the Father. We must look to His love in giving Himself for us to motivate us to want to please Him, and we must look to Him to make our imperfect obedience acceptable to the Father. It is only in this manner that we can please God and glorify Him.

Please note that in all this discussion, I have not mentioned any specific rules of conduct, or what we often call the "dos and don'ts." These have their place and we will look at some of them in the next section. But I have first of all attempted to address our hearts. What do we desire? If we do not desire to do the will of God, if we do not desire to please Him and glorify Him, then the rules of conduct become burdensome. We either ignore them or at best obey them reluctantly and halfheartedly. Or we focus entirely on outward conduct, that by which we remain respectable to other people while ignoring entirely the underlying sins of the heart.

If we truly want to do our part (our dependent responsibility) in being conformed to Christ, we must address the issues of our hearts. When in the depths of our hearts we delight to do the will of God and thus please Him and glorify Him, then the biblical rules of conduct will be more a means of moral guidance than a set of rules we must obey. In fact, we will be eager to know His moral will so that we can please Him by doing it. I don't know if you picked up on it, but in my discussion of serving my wife by doing some ordinary household chores, I said I saw it as an *opportunity* — not an obligation — to love my wife in that way. That is the way we should view all the commandments of Scripture. They present us an unending series of opportunities to express our gratitude to God for His grace to us through Christ.

And now having laid the foundation of the heart, let's turn our attention to some specific details in our daily walk.

OUR DAILY WALK

Anyone who has studied or even carefully read Paul's letter to the Ephesians knows that the letter is easily divided into two parts. In chapters 1–3, Paul delineated what God has done for us in and through Christ. In chapters 4–6, he spelled out what our response of gratitude should be through obedience in specific areas of life. Bible students often refer to this type of division as the indicative and the imperative. The indicative is a statement of fact about what God has done for us, and the imperative spells out, to some degree, how we should live in our response of gratitude.

Accordingly, Paul began the second section of Ephesians with *therefore* — that is, in view of what God has done for us in Christ (the indicative), this is how we should "walk," or live out the ordinary course of our daily lives (the imperative).

Key to this whole section about our daily walk is 4:22-24: "Put off your old self, which belongs to your former manner of life and is corrupt through deceitful desires, and to be renewed in the spirit of your minds, and to put on the new self, created after the likeness of God in true righteousness and holiness." This passage offers what is known as the "put off/put on" principle, an important concept to grasp if we would be conformed to Christ in our daily lives. Basically, we should not only give attention to putting away sinful attitudes and actions in our lives but also strive to put on positive Christlike traits, such as love, humility, compassion, patience, and a forgiving spirit (see Galatians 5:22-23; Colossians 3:12-14). All of these positive traits can be called the fruit of the Spirit, even if they are not listed in Galatians 5:22-23.

My observation is that most believers who grasp the importance of spiritual transformation tend to focus more on the sins we need to put off than the traits we need to put on. Yet Christ said, "By this all people will know that you are my disciples, if you have love for one another" (John 13:35). The watching world is not impressed by what we don't do; rather, people may be more impressed if they see us loving one another and even loving them!

In the verses following Ephesians 4:22-24, Paul gave specific examples of how to apply the "put off/put on" principle. These examples can be grouped into three categories: integrity (see 4:25,28), sexual purity (see 5:3-4), and interpersonal relationships (see 4:26-27,29-32; 5:1-2).

In the first area, that of integrity, Paul mentioned falsehood (see Colossians 3:9) and stealing. It would be easy to pass over these areas, thinking, "I don't do those things." And that is probably true in the more obvious expressions of lying and stealing, but what about the more subtle areas? Do we ever exaggerate the truth to create a false impression, either of ourselves or our accomplishments, or, in the opposite direction, to reflect negatively on another person, church, or organization?

Are we somewhat loose with our facts when reporting an event or telling a story? Or do we strive to "tell the truth, the whole truth, and nothing but the truth"? It may seem as if I'm dealing with ethical minutia here, but, to borrow words from Song of Solomon 2:15, it is "the little foxes that spoil the vineyards." It is the little half-truths or embellishment of facts that can compromise our commitment to absolute integrity.

Hopefully we don't steal in the sense of robbery or shoplifting, but do we ever plagiarize the writings or words of someone else without giving them credit? I once asked a seminary student if cheating ever occurred at seminary. He said, "Oh yes, but it is not cheating on exams. It is plagiarizing by getting papers off the Internet and doctoring them to make them appear as one's own work. And most of these students will one day be pastors!"

Are we scrupulous about our company expense account reports and our income tax returns? I personally find it helpful when working on my tax returns to think of the Holy Spirit as auditing my return. Though I want to be completely honest with the government on my tax returns, it is far more important that I do not sin against God by the entries I make.

A danger of delving into details such as plagiarizing term papers or fudging on tax returns is that I may miss the area or areas of which you are most tempted. We are all tempted in various and different ways, and I hope you will have picked up on the principle of striving for integrity in the little things so that you will be prompted to carefully examine your own life for the "little foxes that spoil the vineyards" of your own integrity. It is also a good idea to ask the Holy Spirit to give you a conscience that is sensitive to the little sins in your life, some that you may not even be aware of.

As to putting on the new man, note the contrast Paul drew between stealing and giving (see Ephesians 4:28). Paul was not content that a person stopped stealing; he exhorted them to be generous — to work so as to be able to share with those in need. Are we generous to give, not only to God's kingdom work so we can take a tax deduction but also to fellow believers who are in need where there is no tax deduction? The apostle John wrote, "If anyone has the world's goods and sees his brother in need, yet closes his heart against him, how does God's love abide in him?" (1 John 3:17). Are we growing in generosity? Are we giving more, both tax deductible and non-tax deductible, as a percentage of our income than we were two or three years ago? If we want to be increasingly conformed to the image of Christ, we must grow in generosity so as to follow His example of becoming poor so that through His poverty we might become rich (see 2 Corinthians 8:9).

The second category Paul addressed is sexual purity. Though Paul's treatment is brief, his message is strong in terms of absolute avoidance of all forms of sexual impurity. We need to examine our habits and activities in this age when sexual activity outside of marriage is accepted as normal by society at large. It is difficult to find a movie, novel, or television drama that does not include illicit sexual activity as a normal part of the story line.

We need to take seriously Jesus' words in Matthew 5:28: "I say to you that everyone who looks at a woman with lustful intent has already committed adultery with her in his heart." A reasonable inference from Jesus' words is that indulging sexual fantasies in one's mind is also committing adultery in one's heart. Therefore, we need to guard our eyes and thoughts as scrupulously as we guard against any physical sexual activity. I don't want to descend into a legalistic set of rules regarding movies, television dramas, and novels, but if we truly want to be conformed to the image of Jesus, we need to think seriously about what we allow our eyes to see and our minds to dwell on.

Sexual purity and the sanctity of marriage are important because God designed human marriage to represent the relationship between Christ and the church. To violate the sanctity of marriage, even in one's heart, is therefore to debase and defile that sacred picture.

It is noteworthy that in Revelation 17, Babylon the great (a code name for Rome) is referred to as "the great prostitute" and "mother of prostitutes" (verses 1,5). Rome was guilty of many egregious sins, including pervasive and gross immorality, wanton luxury, the legal practice of slavery, the deification of the emperor, and the persecution of Christians, yet God uses the image of prostitution to describe the empire in all its degradation. Of all the specific sins — such as lying, stealing, and murder — that God could have used, by calling Rome the great prostitute, He chose the image of sexual immorality to cover them all. Surely this says something to us about God's attitude toward sexual immorality.

Here I need to address an important aside to Christian women and girls. Remember Paul's words in Romans 12:2, "Do not be conformed to this world." There is probably no other area of life in which Christian young women are so prone to be conformed to the world than in their standard of dress. They want to be in fashion, so they buy whatever the latest styles are without regard to whether or not they are modest. But as someone who wants to be conformed to the image of Christ, you cannot afford to do that. You must instead be careful to avoid clothing that attracts the eyes of men. I know this is difficult today when so much of women's clothing is deliberately designed to be provocative, but however long and hard you must look you should seek clothing that is modest. Though you may not realize it, if you wear revealing clothing, you are probably as guilty of sexual impurity as is the man who looks at you with lustful eyes. And a word to parents, both moms and dads: It is your responsibility to ensure that your teenage daughters first of all understand the seriousness of this subject and that as Christians (assuming they are) they should gladly, in response to Christ's love for them, seek to please Him in their dress.

And finally the most major issue today in the subject of sexual purity is Internet pornography. In the mid-fourteenth century, the bubonic plague, called the Black Death, spread rapidly across all of Europe, resulting in the deaths of between 30 and 60 percent of Europe's population. Our term for this is a pandemic, a widespread epidemic. Today we have a moral pandemic in our country. A colleague of mine who ministers to college students and who has studied this subject extensively told me that 98 percent of freshmen men entering the university today are involved to some degree in Internet pornography. And, unbelievably, the figure for freshmen women is 40 percent! He said it does not matter if students are from Christian families, attended Christian high schools, or were homeschooled — the percentages remain unbelievably high.

Of course, men and women of all ages and all stations in life are being swept up into this evil activity, so it is not an overstatement to call this phenomenon a moral pandemic. It is well known that the annual revenue from Internet pornography exceeds the combined revenues of the National Football League, the National Basketball Association, and Major League Baseball. Truly our country is awash in this moral filth.

This subject is so big and so complex that it is beyond the scope of this book to address our response to this issue. But the evangelical church, Christian high schools and colleges, and parents must address the moral cancer in our society. Otherwise, we are leaving our young people, our next generation of parents, exposed and defenseless before what is probably the greatest moral threat our country has ever faced.

The third area of "put off/put on" that Paul dealt with is interpersonal relationships. This is an area to which most of us need to give attention. We might pass by Paul's exhortations on integrity and sexual purity with the assumption we have no problems in those areas, but who of us can plead completely innocent in the way we treat one another?

I have known people who appeared to be completely above reproach in the areas of integrity and sexual purity but who were judgmental, self-righteous, and even harsh in their relationships with other people. Yet as important as are the areas of integrity and sexual purity, Paul gave more emphasis to this area than to the other two combined. In the edition of the Bible I use, sixteen lines of print from Ephesians 4:25 through 5:4 deal with interpersonal relationships, while eleven lines are devoted to integrity and sexual purity combined. This comparison is by no means intended to diminish the importance of integrity or sexual purity but to point out how important interpersonal relationships are.

This whole section on interpersonal relationships is worthy of our prayerful, thoughtful reflection, and I urge you to open your Bible to Ephesians 4:25–5:4 and pray over each aspect, asking God to reveal to you any attitude or action that needs to be put off or any one you need to grow in.

Anger is the first sinful attitude Paul mentioned. Here we need to take seriously the warning of Jesus in Matthew 5:22, "Everyone who is angry with his brother will be liable to judgment." Anger among believers most often expresses itself in harsh speech by which we express our extreme displeasure at the attitude, words, or actions of another person.

I think of the words of James in connection with sins of the tongue: "With [the tongue] we curse people who are made in the likeness of God" (3:9). To curse someone is not limited to profanity; it means any kind of imprecatory language by which we express ill will toward someone else.

God uses a similar expression in Genesis 9:6: Murder is forbidden because "God made man in his own image." Murder and angry speech are both sins because they are directed toward someone who is created in the image of God. And then when we realize that Jesus said that both murder and anger will make us liable to judgment (see Matthew 5:21-22), we should begin to realize what a serious sin our anger is.

Is there a place then for righteous anger? Of course there is. But too often we tend to excuse our sinful anger under the guise of righteous indignation. If our anger is a reaction to words or actions directed toward us, then our anger is probably sinful anger.

Other interpersonal sins to put off include bitterness, wrath, anger (fury), clamor, and slander (see Ephesians 4:31). All of these are sinful attitudes and speech growing out of the anger we have just discussed. They are, in a sense, various expressions of anger carried to a higher level. We can see here the destructive force of anger and begin to understand why it is a major sin along with lying, stealing, and sexual impurity of any kind.

But we are not to simply put off anger and its related sins; instead, we are to "be kind to one another, tenderhearted, forgiving one another as God in Christ forgave [us]" (verse 32). As God's forgiveness of us is the key to understanding forgiveness, Jesus once told a parable about a servant who owed his master ten thousand talents (based on a wage of $40,000 a year, that would be about eight billion dollars in today's currency). When he could not pay, the master freely forgave him of the debt. Shortly thereafter, the forgiven servant met another servant who owed him a hundred denarii (about ten to fifteen thousand dollars for today's workman) and refused to forgive him.

The master called the first servant back to him and said, "You wicked servant! I forgave you all that debt because you pleaded with me. And should not you have had mercy on your fellow servant, as I had mercy on you?" (Matthew 18:32-33). The application should be clear to us. All of us are represented by the first servant. We are all ten-thousand-talent debtors. We each owe God a moral and spiritual debt we could not possibly pay. But God in Christ — that is, through the death of Christ — forgave us. And Paul said that we are to forgive one another as God forgave us.

Is there anyone toward whom you are nursing an unforgiving spirit? Perhaps it is over an incident that occurred several years ago or even longer and you never truly forgave. The details and your reaction at that time may now lie buried in the back of your mind, but from time to time something triggers your memory about it, and the old unforgiving spirit arises again. If this is true, that spirit is hindering you from becoming conformed to the image of Christ.

God said in Isaiah 43:25, "I will not remember your sins" (see also Hebrews 8:12; 10:17). To not remember means we choose not to bring up old wounds from other people, either to ourselves or another person. And when they do come into our minds unbidden, we immediately put them away.

Most of us need to pay particular attention to Paul's admonition regarding our speech (see Ephesians 4:29). Again Paul used absolute language: *no* corrupting talk, *only* such as is good for building others up. Corrupting talk is any speech that tends to tear down another person, either someone we are talking to or someone we are talking about. When talking to someone, this would include words spoken out of anger or impatience, sarcasm, or any words designed to put down the person we are talking to. When talking *about* someone, it includes gossip, slander, or any speech calculated to negatively reflect on the character or actions of that person.

In the very next verse, Paul wrote, "Do not grieve the Holy Spirit of God." I'm confident that all sin grieves the Holy Spirit and I think that warning would have been appropriate in either the areas of integrity or sexual purity. However, Paul, writing under the infallible guidance of the Holy Spirit, chose to include it immediately after his exhortation about our speech. I think this says something to us. We would all agree that a lack of integrity or any sexual impurity or even our sinful anger grieves the Holy Spirit. But are we willing to face the fact that any corrupting speech, either to or about someone, also grieves the Holy Spirit? Elsewhere, Paul wrote that we are to "speak evil of no one" (Titus 3:2). The sad truth for most of us is that negative speech about someone else seems to slide off our tongues as naturally as eating. I can't tell you how many times I have to check myself and refrain from saying something just "slightly" negative about another person.

Are we willing to make Titus 3:2 our goal as we seek to be conformed to the likeness of Christ? If you are, let me suggest three questions you can ask yourself about your speech to or about others:

- Is it true?
- Is it kind?
- Is it necessary?

If what you are about to say, either to or about someone, cannot pass these three tests, you should refrain from saying it.

Our tongues can be instruments to build up or to tear down. Ask the Holy Spirit to begin making you aware of speech that tends to tear down another person and to enable you to see where you can use your tongue more to build up others. Then ask Him to show you critical attitudes in your heart, for Jesus said, "Out of the abundance of the heart the mouth speaks" (Matthew 12:34).

We've covered a lot of territory in this chapter, so let me first give attention to the attitude of our hearts. Do we desire to do the will of God, to please Him and glorify Him? This is much more effective than focusing only on outward conduct. In fact, without a heart to do the will of God, outward conduct change is only superficial. Second, remember it is just as important to put on positive Christlike character as it is to deal with persistent sin patterns in our lives.

In the area of specific sins, I want to highlight three of them:

- The importance of absolute sexual purity
- The seriousness of sinful anger
- The need to watch critical speech to or about someone else

Above all, "Keep your heart with all vigilance, for from it flow the springs of life" (Proverbs 4:23).

FOR GROUP DISCUSSION

1. What kind of gratitude causes us to *want* to do what we *ought* to do? How does this play out in day-to-day, moment-by-moment life?
2. Do you think Jesus' words in Matthew 5:28 apply to pornography use and to thought-life issues such as sexual fantasy? Why or why not?
3. Referring to Matthew 18:21-35, what is meant by the expression "We are all ten-thousand-talent debtors"?

CHAPTER FOURTEEN

Already, Not Yet!

As obedient children, do not be conformed to the passions
of your former ignorance, but as he who called you is holy,
you also be holy in all your conduct, since it is written,
"You shall be holy, for I am holy."

1 PETER 1:14-16

G od commands us to be holy. He said, "You shall be holy, for
I am holy." So God has predestined us to be conformed to
the image of His Son, and He has commanded us to be holy as He
is holy. Conformity to the image of Christ and being holy as God
is holy are essentially synonymous expressions. What God has
purposed for us, He commands that we pursue.

This command is incumbent on all believers, not just a group
of super-spiritual people or full-time Christian workers. It is for
the high school student as well as the young adult in college or in
the workplace. It includes the stay-at-home mom and the person
in the professional and business world and, yes, even the retiree
enjoying the leisure of later years. It applies to all believers. It
allows no exceptions.

The New Testament is replete with calls to holiness. Consider
the following Scriptures:

- Since we have these promises, beloved, let us cleanse ourselves from every defilement of body and spirit, bringing holiness to completion in the fear of God. (2 Corinthians 7:1)
- Put on the new self, created after the likeness of God in true righteousness and holiness. (Ephesians 4:24)
- God has not called us for impurity, but in holiness. (1 Thessalonians 4:7)
- They disciplined us for a short time as it seemed best to them, but he disciplines us for our good, that we may share his holiness. (Hebrews 12:10)
- Strive for peace with everyone, and for the holiness without which no one will see the Lord. (Hebrews 12:14)
- Since all these things are thus to be dissolved, what sort of people ought you to be in lives of holiness and godliness. (2 Peter 3:11)

The truth is that all the moral imperatives in the Bible are calls to holiness, so we are to pursue holiness with all the vigor and intentionality the word *pursue* suggests.

AN OUTWARD FOCUS

At the same time, however, we must guard against looking inward and becoming preoccupied with our own spiritual transformation. On the evening of His resurrection day, Jesus said to His disciples, "As the Father has sent me, even so I am sending you" (John 20:21). Though these words were spoken to His disciples, they are applicable to us today, both corporately as the body of Christ and individually. There is a sense in which Jesus is saying to each one of us, "As the Father has sent me, even so I am sending you." To be conformed to the image of Christ, then, involves not only transformation of our character but also involvement in

Christ's mission to the world. Just as the moral command to be holy as God is holy applies to all believers, so Jesus' words "So send I you" apply to all of us without exception.

This obviously does not mean that every believer is to be a missionary or any other form of full-time vocational Christian work. It does mean that each of us has a role, either directly or indirectly. The Bible is clear that every Christian has received at least one spiritual gift (see 1 Peter 4:10-11; 1 Corinthians 12:4-11; Romans 12:4-8). A spiritual gift is an ability given and empowered by the Holy Spirit to enable a person to fulfill his or her function within the body of Christ. And the fact that all of us have received a gift means that all of us have a function to fulfill. As Paul said in Ephesians 2:10, "We are his workmanship, created in Christ Jesus for good works, which God prepared beforehand, that we should walk in them." To paraphrase and greatly condense Paul's words in Ephesians 2:8-10, "We are not saved *by* works, but we are saved *to* works, to do the work God has prepared for us to do."[1]

Every believer has a role to play in carrying out Christ's Great Commission to make disciples of all nations (see Matthew 28:18-20). Obviously, we are not all to go to other nations or cultures, but we can all partner with those who do go, through our prayer, encouragement, and financial support. For many of us, our primary work in the body will be behind the scenes, making it possible for those on the front lines of Christ's mission to the world to be more effective. But whether our function in the body and in the fulfillment of the Great Commission is visible or invisible, all of us have a role to fulfill. And to be more conformed to Christ means we take our role just as seriously as we do our character transformation.

WORDS OF ENCOURAGEMENT

Having looked briefly at the importance of the outward missional focus that should be true of all believers, I want to return now to the main purpose of *this* book, which is the transformation of our character so that we become increasingly conformed to the image of Christ. And as I do this, I want to encourage you to persevere in this pursuit, even when you think you are not making much progress. The truth is that the more sincerely and diligently we pursue holiness, the more sin and character flaws we will see in our own lives. The reason for this is twofold.

First, the Holy Spirit does not show us all our sin at once. Rather, He gradually shows us from the Scriptures what it means to have Christlike character and enables us to see where we fall short of it. It is not (I hope) that we are sinning more; it is that we are becoming more aware of and more sensitive to sin that has been there all along.

Second, as long as we live, we experience the internal fighting that Paul described in Galatians 5:17: "The desires of the flesh are against the Spirit, and the desires of the Spirit are against the flesh, for these are opposed to each other, to keep you from doing the things you want to do." More than 150 years ago, Scottish theologian George Smeaton wrote,

> There [is] an internal conflict between flesh and spirit.... And the strange thing is that in this conflict, the powers and faculties of the Christian seem to be occupied at one time by the one and at another time by the other. The same intellect, will and affections come under different influences like two conflicting armies occupying the ground and in turn driven from the field. To the astonishment of the Christian himself, the mind and affections engaged in the exercises of holy love by the power of the Holy Spirit may all of a sudden be turned away by some root of sin or strange law of association in the mental economy to the very opposite. Thus, the conflict continues to the end. We may compare it — though no analogy can exactly portray it — to one in a state of convalescence

where disease and health are struggling for the mastery, sometimes the one predominating and sometimes the other, till the disease is fully and forever expelled from the veins.[2]

We should keep in mind that we live in what theologians call the "already, not yet" era between Christ's ascension and His second coming. During this time, there is a continual tension between who we are "in Christ" and what we are in our daily experience. Through our union with Christ, we are already seated with Him in the heavenly places (see Ephesians 2:6), yet we still live in a sin-cursed world with all its difficulties and pain. We are already holy and blameless before God through our union with Christ (see Ephesians 1:4), but we still sin every day.

In dealing with our sin, I find it helpful to think of four areas:

- The guilt of sin
- The reign of sin
- The presence of sin (the flesh)
- The activity of sin

All four of these facets of sin are common to all unbelievers. They were true of each of us before we trusted in Christ as our Savior. We were under the guilt of sin and, as a consequence, we were under its reign. We could not please God. Paul said, "Those who are in the flesh cannot please God" (Romans 8:8). We might have been nice, decent individuals, but even at our best, nothing we did while outside of Christ could please God.

When we trust in Christ as our Savior, we are, through His death, forgiven of our sin so that we are no longer considered guilty before God. He has forgiven us all our sin because Jesus bore that sin on the cross (see Colossians 2:13; 1 Peter 2:24). Having then been freed from the guilt of sin, we are, as a result, freed from its reign in our lives. As Paul put it in Romans 6:2, we have "died to sin" — not to its activity in our lives but to its absolute reign. Sin may wage its guerilla warfare against us, but it cannot reign in our lives. We have, to use Paul's words, died to that reign.

So we no longer have a relationship to sin's guilt and reign, but we still have the presence of the flesh to deal with. When we want to do right, evil (that is, the flesh) lies close at hand (see Romans 7:21). The fact that we still experience the presence and struggle of sin is part of the "already, not yet" tension of this life.

Because we still have the flesh waging war against us, we still experience the *activity* of sin every day. But we are called on to put it to death (see Colossians 3:5). We are to abstain from the passions of the flesh that war against our souls (see 1 Peter 2:11). People without Christ do not experience this warfare; they live comfortably under sin's reign. But once we are delivered from that reign, the warfare with sin begins. I call this the discomfort of the justified state. On the one hand, we are justified. As we saw in chapter 4, we stand before God just as if we'd never sinned and just as if we had always obeyed. On the other hand, we see that, in our daily experience, we *do* sin; we often *do not* obey.

So what will keep us from becoming discouraged as we see further sin in our lives? What will motivate us to persevere in our battle with remaining sin, even on those days when we don't seem to make any progress? It is the realization that in Christ we already stand holy and blameless before God.

If you commit yourself to the pursuit of Christlikeness, you will discover an increasing tension between your desire to know and do the will of God and your perceived progress in doing it. This increased tension can become discouraging and demotivating. The solution to this dilemma is to keep in mind that, in our standing before God, He sees us clothed in the perfect obedience of Christ. This standing never changes, regardless of whether we are having a good day or a bad day. In Him, we are always holy and blameless. In Him, we are always as perfectly righteous as He was in His sinless humanity.

This is the way we should resolve the tension between what we desire to be and what we see of ourselves in our daily experience. We should look more at our standing before God in Christ than we do at our actual experience, and that continual looking to who we are in Him will motivate us to become more like Him in our experience. To do this, of course, means we must daily embrace the gospel.

So to summarize this book, let me give you seven characteristics of a person who is pursuing holiness — a person who is becoming more conformed to the image of Christ. This person has:

1. A growing understanding of the holiness of God and its implications for us.
2. A growing sensitivity to remaining sinfulness and a concurrent realization of failure to more fully express the fruit of the Spirit in one's life.
3. An earnest desire and a sincere effort to grow in Christlikeness, realizing that desire will always exceed fulfillment.
4. A clear understanding of the principle of dependent responsibility and how to apply that principle in one's life.
5. A consistent application of the instruments of grace through the practice of the spiritual disciplines, which enables us to grow in Christlikeness.
6. A continual embracing of the gospel for the assurance of forgiveness of our sins and of our righteous standing before God so that we will be constrained by His love to live, not for ourselves but for Him.
7. A growing realization of one's own spiritual inability and an increasing dependence on the Holy Spirit to work in us and enable us to work.

Even though the sixth characteristic is listed as one of seven, it should actually permeate all the previous five.

We cannot truly grow in our understanding of the infinite holiness of God and the exceeding sinfulness of our sin unless we view His holiness and our sin through the lens of the gospel. To view them apart from the gospel only produces a "woe is me" mindset instead of a joyous "Here am I, send me" attitude. And the earnest desire and sincere effort of the third characteristic (the "pressing on" of Paul in Philippians 3:12-14) can be maintained only through the motivation of the gospel. The same is true of the practice of the spiritual disciplines.

A growing sense of one's own spiritual inability and an increasing dependence on the Holy Spirit should also permeate the first five characteristics. Only the Holy Spirit can truly give us a growing understanding of the holiness of God and an increased awareness of our own sinfulness. He does this primarily through His Word, but without His enlightening and convicting powers, our knowledge of the Scriptures will remain merely intellectual. We need His powerful action to drive home to our hearts an increasing experiential knowledge of these truths. In a similar manner, we are dependent on the Holy Spirit to enable us to effectively practice the spiritual disciplines and to see them as "instruments of grace" given for our benefit rather than mere duties to practice in order to earn God's favor.

As long as we live in the "already, not yet" era, we will continue to be at war with the world, the Devil, and our own sinful flesh. Though the final victory in this warfare is assured, we do experience defeats and setbacks as we sin, so we must keep our eyes on Jesus and His sinless life and sin-bearing death through which we stand always before God clothed in the perfect righteousness of Christ. And we must continually look to the Holy Spirit to empower us in this warfare. The righteousness of Christ and the power of the Holy Spirit are the two foundation stones upon which spiritual transformation is built.

Finally, we can look forward to the day when at death we enter into the presence of the Lord and be among "the spirits of the righteous made perfect" (Hebrews 12:23). Beyond that, "we know that when he appears [at the Second Coming] we shall be like him, because we shall see him as he is" (1 John 3:2). And then John added, "And everyone who thus hopes in him purifies himself as he is pure" (verse 3). May this be true of us!

FOR GROUP DISCUSSION

1. The more sincerely and diligently we pursue holiness, the more we will see our sins and character flaws. What are two reasons for this?
2. Four components of sin are listed here. How do unbelievers and believers experience these differently?
   a. The guilt of sin
   b. The reign of sin
   c. The presence of sin (the flesh)
   d. The activity of sin
3. What will keep us from becoming discouraged as we see more and more sin in our lives? What will motivate us to persevere in our battle with remaining sin, even on those days when we don't seem to make any progress? Fill in the blank in this key sentence referring to "already, not yet": "It is the realization that in Christ we already stand _____ and _____ before God."

Notes

CHAPTER TWO: **The Holiness of God**

1. J. Alec Motyer, *The Prophecy of Isaiah* (Downers Grove, IL: InterVarsity, 1993), 77.

2. Edward J. Young, *The Book of Isaiah* (Grand Rapids, MI: Eerdmans, 1965), 242.

3. It is noteworthy that when the apostle John saw a vision of God seated on His throne, he also heard angelic creatures crying out, "Holy, holy, holy, is the Lord God Almighty" (see Revelation 4:1-8). Some eight hundred years separated the visions of Isaiah and John. It is reasonable to assume that when God created angels in the depths of eternity and reaching forward to an eternal duration, there has always been and will always be heavenly creatures constantly calling out, "Holy, holy, holy, is the Lord."

4. William Plumer, *Psalms* (1867; repr., Edinburgh, Scotland: Banner of Truth Trust, 1975), 557.

5. George Smeaton, *Christ's Doctrine of the Atonement* (1870; repr., Edinburgh, Scotland: Banner of Truth Trust, 1991), 21.

6. I am indebted to my friend Bill Vogler for the idea of this illustration.

CHAPTER THREE: **The Sinfulness of Our Sin**

1. J. Alec Motyer, *The Prophecy of Isaiah* (Downers Grove, IL: InterVarsity, 1993), 78, 430.

2. F. F. Bruce, *The Epistle to the Hebrews,* The New International Commentary on the New Testament (Grand Rapids, MI: Eerdmans, 1990), 336.
3. James Buchanan, *The Doctrine of Justification* (1867; repr., Edinburg, Scotland: Banner of Truth Trust, 1961), 236–237.

CHAPTER FOUR: **The Great Exchange**

1. Philip E. Hughes, *The Second Epistle to the Corinthians*, The New International Commentary on the New Testament (Grand Rapids, MI: Eerdmans, 1962), 211.
2. Charles Hodge, *Second Epistle to the Corinthians* (London: Banner of Truth Trust, 1959), 150.

CHAPTER FIVE: **A Daily Embracing of the Gospel**

1. Richard Lovelace, *Dynamics of Spiritual Life* (Downers Grove, IL: InterVarsity, 1979), 101.
2. Lovelace, 101.
3. "Miserable Sinner Christianity," *Works of B. B. Warfield*, vol. 7 (Grand Rapids, MI: Baker, 1991), 113ff.
4. Robert Haldane, *Exposition of the Epistle to the Romans* (1874; repr., Edinburgh, Scotland: Banner of Truth Trust, 1958), 132.
5. Taken from John Owen, *Communion with the Triune God,* edited by Kelly M. Kapic and Justin Taylor, ©2007, 316–319. Used by permission of Crossway, a publishing ministry of Good News Publishers, Wheaton, IL 60187, www.crossway.org.

CHAPTER SIX: **The Motivation of the Gospel**

1. On the basis of John's words in John 12:37-41, some Bible scholars believe that the Lord sitting on the throne of Isaiah 6:1 was actually the preincarnate Son of God. They believe this because of the way John linked the quotation from Isaiah 6:9-10 with his statement that "Isaiah said these things because he saw his glory and spoke of him" (John 12:41).

2. Norval Geldenhuys, *Commentary on the Gospel of Luke*, The New International Commentary on the New Testament (Grand Rapids, MI: 1977), 234.
3. J. C. Ryle, *Holiness* (Old Tappan, NJ: Revell, n.d.), 88.
4. Kenneth S. Wuest, *The New Testament: An Expanded Translation* (Grand Rapids, MI: Eerdmans, 1961), 424.
5. John Newton, "Hymn 3," Christian Classics Ethereal Library, www.ccel.org/ccel/newton/olneyhymns.h3_3.html. (This quote was first brought to my attention by Timothy Keller in *The Prodigal God* [New York: Dutton, 2008], 88–89).
6. William Cowper, "Love Constrained to Obedience," Poets' Corner, http://theothers.org/poems/olney03.html. (This quote was first brought to my attention by Timothy Keller in *The Prodigal God*, 88–89).

CHAPTER SEVEN: **Understanding God's Grace**

1. Archibald Alexander, *Thoughts On Religious Experience* (Edinburg, Scotland: Banner of Truth Trust, 1967), 165.
2. C. FitzSimons Allison, *The Rise of Moralism* (Vancouver, Canada: Regent College Press, 2003).
3. Alexander, 165.
4. This quote is from memory from an article written some years ago, but when I read it, it "burned" in my soul, and I've never forgotten it.
5. Charles Spurgeon, quoted in Iain Murray, *Spurgeon v. Hyper-Calvinism* (Carlisle, PA: Banner of Truth Trust, 1995), 20.
6. John Owen, *Communion with God,* ed. R. J. K. Law (Edinburgh, Scotland: Banner of Truth Trust, 1991), 117.
7. Lefèvre d'Étaples, quoted in Philip Hughes, *A Commentary on the Epistle to the Hebrews* (Grand Rapids, MI: Eerdmans, 1977), 461.
8. Martin Bucer, quoted in Hughes, 461.

CHAPTER NINE: Dependent Responsibility

1. John Owen, *The Holy Spirit* (Evansville, IN: Sovereign Grace Publisher, 1960), 228.
2. Jonathan Edwards, *The Works of Jonathan Edwards*, vol. 1 (Edinburgh, Scotland: Banner of Truth Trust, 1979).
3. Edwards.
4. Iain H. Murray, *Jonathan Edwards: A New Biography* (Carlisle, PA: Banner of Truth Trust, 1987), 101.

CHAPTER TEN: Instruments of Grace

1. Philip E. Hughes, *The Second Epistle to the Corinthians* (Grand Rapids, MI: Eerdmans, 1962), 117–118.
2. John Calvin, *Institutes of the Christian Religion*, vol. 1 (Philadelphia: Westminster, 1960), 566.
3. James Fraser, *A Treatise on Sanctification* (Audubon, NJ: Old Paths Publications, 1992), 463.
4. James Buchanan, *The Office and Work of the Holy Spirit* (Carlisle, PA: Banner of Truth Trust, 1966), 245.

CHAPTER TWELVE: The Grace of Adversity

1. For a more thorough treatment of this subject, see my book *Trusting God: Even When Life Hurts* (NavPress).

CHAPTER FOURTEEN: Already, Not Yet!

1. For an extensive discussion of spiritual gifts and particularly how to discern one's gifts, see my book *True Community* (NavPress, 2012), chapter 7, "Spiritual Gifts Within the Community."
2. George Smeaton, *The Doctrine of the Holy Spirit* (Carlisle, PA: Banner of Truth Trust, 1958), 228.

About the Author

J erry Bridges is an author and Bible teacher. His most popular book, *The Pursuit of Holiness,* has sold over one million copies. He is also the author of *Respectable Sins, Trusting God, The Discipline of Grace, The Practice of Godliness, The Fruitful Life,* and *The Gospel for Real Life.* As a full-time staff member with The Navigators for many years, Jerry now serves in the collegiate ministry, in staff development, and as a resource to collegiate ministry staff.

More Timeless Classics . . .

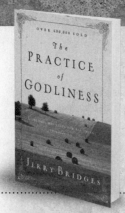

The Practice of Godliness
Jerry Bridges

In this book, Jerry Bridges examines what it means to grow in Christian character. Learn more about the character of God as you grow a deeper relationship with Him. Establish the foundation upon which godly character is built and continue by developing maturity and pursuing holiness.

978-0-89109-941-3

The Discipline of Grace
Jerry Bridges

Explore how the same grace that brings us to faith in Christ also disciplines us in Christ. *The Discipline of Grace* offers a clear and thorough explanation of the gospel and what it means to be a believer.

978-1-57683-989-8

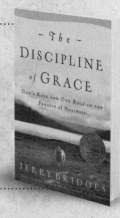

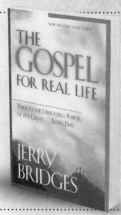

The Gospel for Real Life
Jerry Bridges

The gospel provides for our eternal salvation, but how does it benefit us day to day? Find out how the gospel sets you free from sin's defeat and daily transforms you into Christlikeness.

978-1-57683-507-4

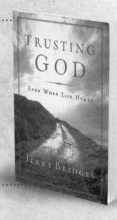